All My Friends

All My Friends:

Charles Carter Renshaw II

Lisa Whiting Renshaw, Editor

Rattlesnake Charlie Publishing
2018

First Printing: 2018

ISBN 978-1-387-93111-8

Rattlesnake Charlie Publishing Company
487 Delwood Court
Newbury Park, CA 91320

Dedication

For my Father on his 90th Birthday. You taught us to love all creatures, so for your Birthday I am immortalizing your stories

Editors Notes and Acknowledgements

My father had no idea I rescued these stories off his ancient, non-internet-connected, no-USB computer. He wrote them decades ago and had I not found some equally ancient, fossilized floppy disks to fetch them into the future, these tales would have been lost.

Now some people may read them and think that's a good thing because many of these tales take place when sexism and homophobia were rampant in our world. It made me chuckle, especially while reading the Poodle Chapter. Our dad a homophobic sexist? Maybe once upon a time when he was a green lad or fresh faced Marine right off the Farm, but I'm happy to say he evolved. My sister and I can vouch that never was there a Dad who empowered his girls more than ours, and as an Attorney he frequently defended the weak and/or persecuted. So I hope you readers can look past any present day comparisons, laugh as I did and enjoy these tales (or is it tails?)

I'd also like to thank my cousin, Jackie Buckley, for proofreading and catching some real zingers for me. Amazing how your brain fills in the blanks and mistakes once you get immersed in a project. Jack I couldn't have finished this on time without your fresh eyeballs, sharp brain, and excellent suggestions.

Finally I'd like to thank my mom "Elynor City Gal" Renshaw and my sister Beth. Beth spurred me on in thinking this was a great idea and that I HAD to do get it done… without that impetus I might not have finished in time for the Big 9-0. As for Mom, these stories wouldn't exist without her. The "Odd Couple" that is my parents is the fuel for most of these tales. She is a proper Boston-bred lady and he will always be a farmer at heart... but that's where the fun comes from!

May everyone who reads this book be reminded of a "Friend" who was dear to them and touched their heart.

Contents

Chapter 1: Country Boy

My first memories begin with events that occurred when I was three or four years old, during the early 1930's. My family consisted of an older sister, my father and mother, and our paternal grandfather who lived with us on a permanent basis.

We lived on a dairy farm in southeastern Pennsylvania, consisting of about 130 acres of rolling land, most of which was used as pasture or under cultivation. Around the fringes of the farm were hardwood forests containing a wide variety of trees and shrubs and which provided a natural habitat for an assortment of wildlife. It was a very rural area and, all in all, provided me with an opportunity to grow from infancy to a young adult in a setting rich with animal friends and close to nature. I feel, as I look back on those early days, I was very fortunate to have grown up as a country boy.

Our main source of cash money came from our herd of Guernsey and Jersey cows. They did not produce, on the average, the quantity of milk that some other breeds did, but they did produce milk of a higher quality that was much richer in its butter fat content. We sold this to a distributor as raw milk.

During the early years, a period that coincided with the beginning of the great depression, and when cash money was in short supply, we did not have a tractor and relied upon draft horses to pull the various items of farm equipment, such as plows, mowers, wagons and our manure spreader. There are those among my human friends who have expressed the opinion that with me on the farm we probably didn't need a manure spreader.

One of the great benefits of living as we did was that we grew virtually all of our own food, both for the family and our animals. In addition to the cows and horses, we raised pigs, goats, chickens, ducks, geese and guinea hens. Money may have been short but solid, nourishing food was not.

All of this, in addition to supplying the memories of my earliest friends, provided a life rich with many lessons for a young boy born in 1928. Needless to say, I did not need any classroom instructions regarding the birds and the bees. The reproductive process was virtually a daily fact of life.

There was, of course, one drawback to this idyllic state of affairs. Notwithstanding my broad education into the wonders and mysteries of life, that education did not extend to an understanding of the female *homo sapiens*. Living on a farm, remote from any intensive association with these baffling creatures, resulted in a case of extreme shyness that continued until my deflowering at the age of 20 years.

I suspect, as I look back now, that I have many sharper memories of all my animal friends as a result of growing up somewhat isolated from my female contemporaries, and on the balance, I am the winner.

The stories I intend to tell you are of of the memories of the pets and animals that I have known for as far back as I can recall through the present. I refer to them as my friends and, indeed, most of them were. In retrospect, while others seem to be friends today, they certainly were not in actual fact, and several can best be described as blood enemies. As you will learn, however, I was the more culpable in the creation of such enmity in most of the cases where it arose, and deserved justly that which was given me.

Before completion of this introductory section, I should tell you that, in addition to all of the other farm animals, we bred, raised and trained horses for riding, showing and fox hunting. My earliest memories are that I started riding at age three-and-a-half. I entered my first show the summer I turned four and, by age six, I was jumping fences with my pony and riding after the fox hounds.

This part of the country produces four distinctive seasons, spring, summer, fall and winter, unlike southern California where life seems to ooze gradually from one season into the next.

Spring and summer were my favorite periods. Spring because, among other things, it meant I would soon be free of school and the drudgery of homework, and summer because I was released from such bondage.

In addition, these were the months that provided the greatest opportunity to enjoy all my friends. It was when the young of almost all the critters arrived, both domestic and wild.

There's just something special about the arrival of spring in that part of the country. As the frost comes out of the ground and the earth is turned over by the first of the year's plowings, there's a musky scent in the air, that is enriched with the perfume of the early flowers on the fruit trees. There's a softness in the winds and you can just sense a stirring of life in general, a quickening as the critters shake off the grip of winter's cold.

The fall of the year, when the leaves begin to turn color, and when the summer's heat has gone, also is a great time to be on the farm. True, it means a return to the evils of education but, freed from the oppressive heat and humidity of summer, life loses the lethargy of August and picks up a faster pace. It is the time of harvest. The smell of burning leaves fills the air.

The only good things I remember about winters are that they provided sledding and ice skating and, if I was lucky, times when we would get so much drifting snow we were unable to leave the farm. That meant no school, and more time to enjoy my dog friends. Unlike a lot of the other critters, dogs are four season friends and continue to give their love and loyalty year round. All in all, they are the best of friends.

Carolyn Hurd Renshaw (mother of Charles) on "Piney," one of Hidden Farms jumpers

All My Friends

Barn Rats!

Chapter 2: Taffy was a Welshman, Taffy was a Thief

We had two Welsh ponies, a mother named Fanny and her son, who was gelded, named Taffy. My father, upon acquiring this pair of equine devils, had also purchased a two-wheeled cart, with rattan, or wicker sides and a rear-end trap door for entry. Of the two ponies, only Fanny was harnessed to pull the cart. I can't say that Taffy wasn't capable of learning this most useful of pony-like chores, only that he did not do so. I think the ability was there, but his nature was such that it never happened. It may seem a paradox that I include Fanny and Taffy as among my friends because, in truth, they were bull-headed, stiff-necked, ornery and, on occasion, down right malicious. Generally speaking, horses are dumb animals. Hell, cows are smarter and a pig's intelligence is far greater. But, I suspect that ponies, notwithstanding their smaller size than a horse, have bigger brains than their larger relatives.

Perhaps a little background is needed. The term pony basically covered every equine up to 58 inches. Horses are measured in hands, a hand being 4 inches. Therefore, ponies were horses whose height did not exceed 14 hands and 2 inches. Welch ponies are about 7 hands, two inches, or plus or minus 3 inches. They are compact, thick necked and well-muscled. For kids they are absolutely great primers. Their backs are wide and comfortable. They are close enough to the ground so that when you fall off, you're not likely to get hurt, other than your ego. Because they are such bull-headed, stubborn and devious creatures, they also provide early training in patience and forbearance.

Of the two members of this particular breed, Taffy was way out in front of his mother in displaying all of the worst habits and characteristics of the Welsh. It may be that Fanny, having brought into the world, or having burdened the world, with her son Taffy, felt that she had done enough to revenge herself upon humans. There were many days when I agreed with that possibility.

I do not mean to suggest that Fanny had forever forsworn playing a trick or two should the thought arise. She just didn't work at it the way her son did. Fanny, while she pulled the little cart, did not like to do so and finally, after several years, wreaked revenge upon it.

Both mother and son could have put a cat burglar to shame. They had an uncanny ability to escape any confinement short of the Federal vault at Leavenworth. All of us spent a lot of time repeatedly chasing that pair of miscreants around the neighborhood upon the occasion of their many dashes for greener pastures.

Normally our cart, after use was housed in a shed, protected from the elements and whatever. Its half demise resulted when, after use on a Saturday, it was left outside the barn area in a flat parking site near the tack and harness room. Fanny and Taffy had been shut in their stalls. Sometime during the night Fanny, whose lips would make a lock picker green with envy, manipulated the latch, freeing herself and Taffy from confinement, and thereby affording them a night of uninterrupted adventure. Trust me that with that pair it was an opportunity not to be wasted.

We were never sure of the exact sequence of their depredations that evening but the circumstantial evidence, viewed the following morning, indicated that once loose, they first made a meal of all of the wicker siding of the pony cart. A large family of beavers could not have caused such a result.

Incidentally, as a general principal, wicker siding is not as tasty or nourishing as timothy hay, which all of our horses were furnished and these two felons had a full rack in their stall. It must have been the opportunity for revenge that drove Fanny to eat the hated cart. Taffy would have done so for the hell of it. Having not quite developed the techniques of termites, my friends did not eat the wheels, shafts or bed of the cart. They just kicked the living hell out of them. That exercise sharpened their appetites and they proceeded to our vegetable garden where they were captured Sunday morning, happily munching on carrot tops and turnip greens. The havoc inflicted upon the garden nearly resulted in the premature demise of my paternal grandfather, who lived with us, and was the family member primarily involved with its culture. He voted the death penalty and immediate execution. All of the rest of us were convinced that had he been the first to spot my rambunctious friends in the garden that we would have been eating pony meat, peppered with double ought buckshot the rest of the summer. My mother, ever the great pacifier, prevailed and both Fanny and Taffy lived on to enjoy further adventures.

Taffy, who would not pull the cart before its untimely end, could be ridden and would often permit my sister and I to do so. Often, but not always. The structure of his neck gave him a decided advantage over either of us. It was short, thick and highly muscled. This, coupled with a mouth that would have made cast iron seem like soft putty, permitted him, if he so choose, to go wherever he wished no matter what the person riding him desired.

We had a large, 3-acre, paddock area, surrounded by a post and rail fence. This was where we exercised and trained our horses over various types of jumps. The fence posts were tied together with three removable rails, about eight feet in length and evenly spaced about 18 inches apart. To get into this pasture area we would take down the rails, and upon leaving, we were supposed to re-place them. However, like most children, being given to lapses of laziness, we would often replace only the middle rail. This dereliction on our part was seized upon by Taffy to our surprise and mortification.

We had jointly ridden him down to the paddock area. Understand that Taffy would occasionally, and always with ill grace, permit a double load. The inherent surliness of his nature would, on such occasions, become obvious to the least observant.

Taffy viewed our riding him double, as a license to resort to any means of unburdening himself of that indignity and he would spare no effort to lighten the load.

Taffy spied the single rail and, bowing his neck, with a steel grip on his bit, he proceeded to walk right under it, spilling my sister and I, like sacks, on the turf. Ordinarily, I would have whooped with glee to see my sister dumped on her fanny. Like most younger brothers, I viewed her with mixed emotions and I was not totally adverse to her getting her just desserts from time to time. There was, however, no joy in jointly sharing in misadventure.

Once rid of us, Taffy proceeded to munch benevolently on the grass inside the paddock. My sister, outraged at her lost dignity, remounted this son of Satan, intent upon teaching him better manners.

Taffy, if nothing else, was a quick study. He immediately perceived that his stratagem would serve equally as well on one rider as it had with two. He simply walked back under the rail a second time, again causing my sister to unload and, having had enough of this activity, trotted back to the stables, leaving to us the joy of walking home.

We employed a black man, named Tunk Lee, who took care of the riding stock and taught us just about everything we ever learned about riding, jumping and showing. In fact, Lee taught me a whole lot about most things from horses to baseball. He was a first-class baseball pitcher and would pick up a little loose change on Sundays throwing for a local black team. De facto segregation was a way of life in that part of Pennsylvania during the early '30's. Anyway, there was a constant battle of wits between Fanny and Lee. It's a tribute to Lee's inherent intelligence that he was the only person on the whole farm that ever scored a victory over the Welsh. Do not mistake me, it wasn't one sided but, at least he got his licks in, whereas all the rest of us just received abuse and humiliation from those two stubby jewels.

I mentioned that Fanny had a marvelous pair of prehensile lips that she utilized to open her stall door. Her system was to snuffle the bolt into a position that allowed her to slide it out of its receptacle, freeing the door. Given her propensity for mischief, Lee viewed this little trick with disfavor. His solution seemed, initially, ingenious. He drove a nail into the door alongside the bolt and bent it over so that it locked over the bolt arm. This could be freed be twisting the nail. It took Fanny three weeks to master the new technique. Finally, the whole assembly was replaced with one that was fitted with a padlock. Try as she could, Fanny could not break out. She died not long after that. Perhaps from old age or, quite possibly, from a loss of the joy of life. One thing I can guarantee, wherever she went, either to pony heaven or hell, she's giving someone a lively time

Chapter 3: Three Devils on Four Legs

I turned four the summer of 1932, when I first became aware that not all of the various critters on our farm were there for my sole joy and amusement. Comparing the two breeds of dairy animals, a vast chasm existed between the basic personalities of the males. Guernsey bulls were generally larger, laid back, and seemed to view life with an amiable benevolence. I had been repeatedly warned not to take liberties with any of the bovine progenitors, but familiarity breeds contempt. Frequent proximity to bulls, along with more than a normal amount of youthful nonchalance, nearly put paid to the only hope my father had for immortality.

The gentle psyche of the Guernsey was not duplicated in the Jersey. Smaller than their barn mates, the Jersey bulls were plain poison. Mean spirited is a mild characterization. Given the least opportunity, and without provocation, they would charge any two-legged animal with but a single thought in mind, mayhem.

In retrospect, I believe that our Jersey bull was about as nasty as they can get. He certainly convinced me that his baleful view of life in general, could only be lightened by using his horns to separate my parts into as many individual pieces as time would permit.

On a Saturday morning, I went to the stable area, where we had a huge pile of baled straw, for the purpose of building a castle with secret passages, ramparts and a tower from which I could rule supreme.

The interior of the barn was dark and, entering from bright sun, my eyes had not adjusted to the differential in the light. Being intent on the project I had in mind, I did not realize that our bad-tempered snorter had been moved from his usual space and temporarily secured near the straw stack. "Secured" is a word used loosely in this tale.

I had barely started to climb the stack, when I was assisted by a shot to my bottom that damn near made me the first human to reach a free orbit in outer space. It also produced an immediate dampness, some of which came from my eyes and the balance which came from a source I had supposedly outgrown.

The fact is, I was very lucky. All of our bulls and, I'm sure, all domestic bulls, had rings in their noses. These rings, together with chains and stout metal rods, were the means of leading them about with reasonable security. Fortunately for me, upon this occasion of my first venture into free flight, a stout chain had been fastened to the bull's nose ring and the other end secured to a cement post. It was just long enough to permit him to reach me with the end of his nose, but short enough to prevent his hooking me with his stubby horns.

Since this was a Saturday, no one was around the barn. It was not until milking time, in the early evening, that wet, scared and weeping, I was rescued from my perch atop the straw bales. To add to what had been less than a winning day, I received a switching as a reminder that I had been told not to build castles out of straw.

Compared with the boar, who kept us in little piglets, the Jersey bull was a pussy cat. As pigs go, he was huge and, while he didn't have horns, he had a pair of razor sharp tusks that were even more lethal. In today's society, a license would be required to carry such weapons. He was fast, quick and very, very smart. I'm certain that, as with Sir Galahad questing after the Holy Grail, that pig's life was equally dedicated to ripping other life forms, female pigs excepted, into tatters. Married to his exceptional physical attributes was a temperament of unmatched ferocity. If he had been a human, he would have been Jack the Ripper. His disposition was so foul, that on his good days, he could have been a brother to Attila the Hun and, on his normal days, he would have made a perfect commandant for any of the Nazi concentration camps. There wasn't another animal on the farm that he was afraid to tackle, nor were there any, including the humans, that wanted to go one on one with him. The only reason that he had not been reduced to sausage and scrapple was his remarkable reproductive capabilities. The pen where he spent his malevolent days was as close to absolute security as we could erect. Alcatraz wasn't tighter. If there is security on death row, that pig's pen was a model for any prison.

Our main barn was built into the side of a hill, made mostly of native stone in the late 1700's. One of the great sporting events for farm boys was leaping into the hay mows. In our barn, we could climb up on the rafters and plummet down into the hay. It was sort of like flying, ending with a soft landing in the sweet smelling timothy hay. Anyway, to get up to the mows, we would usually walk up behind the barn to the second level, past a large, stone silo, and into the barn. Parked beside the silo was a silage cutting machine that was used to chop up corn fodder for winter feed for the cows. On an afternoon when I was five, my sister and I were headed for the mows for a little recreational jumping. Being a year and half older than I, she easily got to the barn well ahead of me. I was about 20 feet short of the barn doors, close to the cutter, when I heard a snort and a long, loud squeal. Startled, I looked behind me and spotted Sir Pig coming up the hill at a dead run and there was no doubt in my mind that he had me in mind for a little afternoon's fun and frolic. In those early years, I can't profess to have possessed any well-developed athletic ability, but the standing jump I made to get on top of the silage cutter might just have gotten me a berth on our national Olympic team. I don't claim that it had grace or class, just that it was a hell of a hop. Was I scared? You can bet your bippy I was scared. In those days I may have weighed fifty pounds, and from my perch, I was looking down on about four hundred pounds of maniacal pork, that was running around the cutter snorting, squealing and waving a pair of lethal sabers like a Prussian swordsman. He tried whittling the machine down with his ivory hookers but, fortunately, it was made of good, hard metal so that all he really accomplished was to hone them a little sharper. It was a stand-off. He couldn't get at me and I couldn't get off the cutter. My sister, who was born smart, had the barn doors closed and barred. While I thought it ungracious of her, she had sense enough not to sally forth in defense of her little brother. Fortunately for me, she had a mouth and a pair of lungs that, when she got wound up to holler, could propel sound into the next county, and she put them into action. Tunk Lee, led a squad of three of our farm hands, to my rescue. Each was armed with a three-pronged hay fork that had eight foot handles. You think that pig was intimidated? No way. He viewed the whole affair as a chance to really do a little chopping. Those guys fought that miserable porker for a good hour. He couldn't get past the forks but he refused to be driven from the area. No matter how hard my heroes tried to drive him away, he was just too quick and kept circling back to my roost. They finally immobilized him after Lee lassoed him with two ropes, then choked him out and believe it or not, hog-tied him. He was loaded on a skid used for hauling fence wire and returned to his pen with one of our draft horses pulling the barge.

His fence, where he broke out, looked like it had been hit with a panzer tank. My grandfather, who was our pig man, had been grooming another young boar as an ultimate successor to Genghis Kahn and made an immediate decision to accelerate the ascension of the younger shoat to the throne of he-pig. I never enjoyed a pork roast, tough as it was, as much as I did that one.

I was innocent as to the development of the foul natures of the bull and the pig. They were the natural result of years of domestication. Mother Nature can shoulder that responsibility. However, as to the third member of this terrorist gang, both my sister and I, contributed to his pugnaciousness.

Our father decided that we should have goat's milk with our meals, attributing to it higher nutritional values than cow's milk. As with all of his programs, my father would establish the grand policy and delegate implementation to the rest of us. Grandpop was the pig man, and I became the goat man. There's a big difference between milking goats and cows. Cows have a teat you can get a good grip on whereas, with goats, you're lucky to be able to use two fingers and a thumb, especially when they are young. I intensely disliked this chore. The nannies were allowed to roam freely around the area and had to be caught each milking time. This was an activity that they, being the playful little buggers that they were, made the most of. The net result was that, by the time I could get them all caught up for milking, I was already tired and bad-tempered and still faced the task of tweaking their teats, all of which took a considerable amount of time that I could have spent in more pleasurable pursuits, such as loafing around, jumping in the hay, and other equally productive activities.

Naturally, along with the nannies, we had to have a billy goat, and dear old dad had purchased a young one. As he matured, he began to grow a set of horns. My sister and I thought it great sport to grab his little stabbers and haul him around. I don't recall who gave him the name of Rademanthus, but a good guess would be that it was my mother. She had an incredible knack of coming up with names for various animals right out of left field. Anyway, Rademanthus resented our taking liberties with his noble person, especially that bit of grabbing his horns. When he was little, there wasn't much he could do about it other than file away in his memory bank the need to get revenge on his tormentors, I being the principal culprit.

The phrase that "he smells like a goat" can only be appreciated by someone who has had the actual experience of getting a whiff of a fully mature billy on a hot, summer's day. Rademanthus, full grown, could be smelled a half mile, upwind. Compared to that goat, a Korean honey wagon smells like Channel No. 5. Downwind, he could give you the vapors.

Full grown Rademanthus had a magnificent rack of matched stilettos. No more could we play games, pulling him around and tormenting him. The shoe, deservedly, was on the other foot. Because of his size, and lethal potentiality, he was normally penned in a wired enclosure. This didn't bother him since it was large and always supplied with a number of gourmet items upon which he could munch, like twigs, tin cans and weeds even the bugs wouldn't eat. It also gave him time to improve upon his unbelievable odor. I'm not going to tell you how he did that because if I did, this book would be banned in Boston. Goat people know how it's done. The amazing thing is that there are ever any pregnant nanny goats. It never occurred to me before, but maybe they don't have a sense of smell. Rademanthus did not pose the deadly threat that the bull and boar pig did. He was kept in his pen mainly to keep the smell away from the house. It would have turned the whitewash yellow. He would, on occasions, be allowed to roam around freely with the nannies, to their mutual pleasure. It was on one of his free days that he paid me back for the liberties I took when he was a kid.

I was returning from school, having gotten off the bus about a mile from home. From the main road, our farm was reached by a narrow dirt road, its boundary beginning about a half mile in from the surfaced road. I had just reached that point where our fences began when I saw my former playmate galloping across the meadow to join up with me. I knew, by this time, that it was not brotherly love that precipitated our meeting. Once he grew up, I had long since learned to leave him alone. As I still had a ways to go to get to the house, I really saw no need for an escort; Rademanthus, on the other hand, had different ideas. It was obvious that one of those was to see how far he could pitch me through the air. That form of free flight held no interest to me, so I frustrated his plans by climbing on top of the fence. That was fine but, you must understand, that this was a very determined billy goat and, he wasn't prepared to abandon his original plans merely because I perched on the top rail of the fence. As soon as I would descend on the opposite side from him, he would hop through the lower rails and challenge me to a duel. Seeing as how I was armed only with a set of school books, while he had a pair of deadly weapons, I felt his attitude somewhat lacking in sportsmanship. So, declining his invitation, I resumed my safe haven on the top rail. It became obvious, even to me, that that bully billy was not going to let me proceed peacefully, to the house, by the usual route of walking on the ground. This was the day that I reached a fuller appreciation of the tightwire walkers in the circus, because Rademanthus made me go the full half mile on top of the fence, until it ended near the house, where I ran the last hundred yards to safety.

Rademanthus was not punished for his fun, nor did I receive any sympathy from my family. When they all stopped laughing hysterically, I was reminded that what goes around, comes around.

Years later, when I received advanced infantry training in the Marine Corps, at Camp Pendleton, a constant refrain from our instructors was "take the high ground." Well, that particular bit of wisdom I had learned years before in combat with the bull, pig and goat. I'm just lucky those critters couldn't climb.

(Editors Note- one would THINK he would have had enough of GOATS yet decades later "Chastity the Wonder Goat" , a flop eared Nubian, became a member of the family and developed quite the nasty personality once she learned that she wouldn't be allowed in the house!)

Chapter 4: The Colonel

Colonel was as big as a pony could be and not be classified as a horse. He stood fourteen hands, two inches on the button. His chestnut color was solid excepting for a wide, white blaze running from his forelock to his nostrils. By age seven, I had progressed from riding the Welsh monsters and now had a mount that was big time. We had purchased Colonel, as a gelding, when he was about three years old, green broken, and not much more. He was mine to train and, as it turned out, visa-versa. Thank God for Tunk Lee.

The first day I had a chance to work him out in the paddock was a complete victory for Colonel. We had a small stream that meandered through our property until it emptied into the Brandywine River. Part of it ran through the paddock. In places where its banks were low it widened to ten to fifteen feet and was quite shallow. In other areas where it narrowed, and deepened, the banks on one side, or the other, rose to three to four feet with sheer walls cut when the stream was in flood, an event usually occurring in the spring.

Unlike Fanny, and her demon son, Colonel, from day one didn't have a mean bone in his body. Naturally, there were days when he was feeling his oats and he would crow-hop a little just to show his good feeling about the world in general. He had been born out west someplace and bore the scar from a branding iron.

On this initial day of the commencement of our relationship, the plan was a simple one. Just walk him around the paddock and get to know each other. The problem arose because Colonel had been western trained to the little degree he had been trained at all. On our farm, all of our horses were raised in the eastern, or English, school. I had never even seen a western saddle, or bridle, other than in Tom Mix's movies. The differences in Colonel's training and mine initially gave rise to a substantial incompatibility. By and large, a western horse turns from rein pressure on his neck, together with leg pressure. Eastern horses turn by tugging the reins on the side you want to turn. As a result, Colonel didn't have a clue as to what I wanted him to do and, I was left sitting on top of an animal that was virtually out of control. I could get him to start and stop, but whatever direction he chose, was the way we went. Three times, on what turned out to be a long, hot afternoon of frustration, Colonel walked down to the stream where, faced with a three foot bank on the other side, he hopped upward to get on top of the far bank, and three times that resulted in my ending up flat on my rear in the middle of the stream, wet clear through and mad as hell. Lee, fortunately, realized the problem immediately, and when he was able to pick himself off the ground, where he'd fallen down in laughter, he took both of us in hand, for a little serious schooling. His solution was simple. He put a lunge line on Colonel and had me work him in the English manner. It took about three hours a day for the best part of a week to get to the point where both Colonel and I knew we were going in the right direction.

Colonel was a perfect steed for me. Big enough so that eventually, when his schooling was completed, I could, and did, everything with him. He became a first class jumper and performed well in shows and fox hunting. He was extremely well-built, strong, and even-tempered, and he could run like the wind.

On Saturday hunt days, we would often leave the farm at five in the morning to ride to a pre-determined rendezvous with the hounds. Some days, that might be close to home, but most often, it would be ten to fifteen miles away. On a good day's hunt, we wouldn't return until early evening, resulting in a long, hard day for horse and rider.

On one early spring day, when I was eleven, Colonel and I, together with Lee, on one of our mares, were long miles upriver, chasing hounds that were chasing a fox. By mid-afternoon, all of us were hot, dusty and tired. As we clipped along, we came down to a shallow ford where the Brandywine ran six to ten inches deep and spanned, bank to bank, about thirty feet. Both Lee and I pulled up in mid-stream to give the horses a drink. In that area, the river ran clear and clean since we were well upstream from the Milltown that turned it into an ecological disaster downstream. Colonel, logically, looked at the sparkling run around his hocks and decided that a quick dip would be just the thing to freshen him up. Unfortunately, he had not consulted with me before putting his plan into effect. The first inkling I had was when he just plopped down in the water and stretched out. In all the years I had been roaming around the countryside on top of him, he had never given the least hint that he had any experience swimming and, as a result, I was completely surprised when he began to act like Johnny Weissmuller.

The best I could do, given the short period of time within which to take defensive action, was to let out a loud squawk and make a fruitless leap for dry ground. I did not make it but, all in all, it wasn't too bad. The water really did feel good. Just goes to show that Colonel was smarter than I was. He had probably remembered the first day I rode him and, having seen me go into the stream three times, figured I must have known something that he did not.

I have mentioned earlier that horses just aren't very smart. I don't know of another animal that will run back into a burning barn. They are also, basically, very timid creatures. They have incredible vision and that, plus their swiftness, is their primary means of self-protection.

Colonel was, as horses go, easy to work with, and by the time he was aged six or seven he really had it all together. When he wanted to, which was most of the time, he could clear a five-foot jump, and considering that's two inches higher than he was, it made him a tough competitor in any pony class, and right in there in most hunter events.

If he had a fault, it was that he could be a tad on the lazy side and, sometimes, he just didn't feel like jumping. Now most horses, in that frame of mind, will just run up to a fence and balk. A sudden stop like that could leave the rider draped over the top rail like wash on a clothesline. Not my pony. Colonel never balked. His was a simpler solution. He would just run right through whatever was in front of him. In our paddock, we had a jump that was made out of rocks that was twenty-four inches high, then topped with a two-foot diameter telephone pole. Normally my friend would canter up to this obstacle and soar over it with little effort. I guess I forgot to mention that he had a barrel chest, broad and well-muscled. We were all getting ready for the big, annual county horse show, which we hosted. At this point, I've got to suppose that some smart-ass reading this is going to think that by training over our home turf, this gave us a wee advantage over the other entries. Anyway, Colonel and I were going around the course just to sharpen our skills but, for reasons he chose not to impart to me, Colonel just didn't want to handle the rock jump the easy way. He did his usual trick on those rare occasions when he decided he didn't want to jump. He just ran flat into it. A bulldozer would have taken an hour to do what colonel did in mere seconds. He had that pole and rocks flying all over the place, and waded right through the resulting debris. He didn't have a scratch or a bruise. I'd had just about all I could do to stay in the saddle and not join all of the other flying objects that were spinning around. To this day, I find it hard to believe that my friend hadn't mussed a hair. I suppose it's a possibility that he had had some engineering training before he came to live with us and, as a result, knew exactly where to hit that fence without risk to himself. However, given the lack of smarts in horses, it's more probable that he, and I, were just lucky.

I can recall one other time when Colonel pulled his trick of running straight ahead instead of jumping. We were on a long hunt and, in fairness to him, had already gone over a lot of fences. We were coming up on a two section, post and rail fence that had three strand barbed wire tied in on both sides. Colonel veered slightly to the left and ran right through the wire, snapping every stand, without so much as a hair out of place. Lucky, again, I guess.

My sister had a little mare, during these times, about the same size as Colonel. She was not built the way he was, she was more dainty. She couldn't outrun Colonel, nor could she out jump him, but in the walk, trot, canter classes, she was pure silk. My sister, and her filly, would regularly whip us in equitation classes but never over the jumps unless, as seldom happened, Colonel would get pokey and drag his toes, whacking the top rails.

Since both my sister, who had the ridiculous nickname of Mouse, and I thought we were exceptionally fine horsemen (I suppose now I'd have to say horsepersons), we had a game we played with Colonel and the filly. We'd ride down to the paddock bareback and see who could pull the other off our respective pony. I'd like to be able to tell you that Colonel and I whipped the two ladies every time or, even most of the time. Not true. I was blessed with having a tomboy for a sister and she was mean and lean. With regularity, she would dump me on the ground with an evil grin. Now that I think about it Mouse still, as a grandmother, has the same smirk.

I left the farm when I was eighteen to go to college in Colorado. Colonel was fourteen, or so, and still in good health. I sold him to a family that wanted a nice, well-trained pony for their eight-year-old daughter. I would like to think that she was given as much pleasure from having Colonel as a friend, as I was.

Later in my life, after having made a well-reasoned decision, at aged eighteen, to forget about horses, I became re-involved in the horse world with my oldest daughter. Counting the thirty, or so, horses we had at the old farm, and the five that my daughter and I worked with later, none were as fine as the Colonel. I'm not sure where Fanny and Taffy ended up but, if fair is fair, Colonel will be in tall grass forever.

Hidden Farm, West Chester Pennsylvania

All My Friends

Chapter 5: Wild Friends Make Poor Pets

Living, as we did, in a very rural area, we were exposed to a rich variety of natural wild life. Large portions of our farm, and the surrounding land, were clothed in hardwood forests that were a refuge to all manner of birds and animals.

My father, ever a person who leapt at every opportunity to make a damn fool decision, such as acquiring our goats, especially good old billy, first proved the proposition that you can take an animal out of the wild but you can't take the wild out of the animal. Dear old Dad would embark on one of his crazy impulses and let the rest of us mop up the mess he had so thoughtfully thrust upon us.

I don't remember, at this time, how, when or why, he acquired the turkey buzzard, nor have I a clue as to the thought process (if in fact there had been one) that led my father to believe that our happy little farm family needed, in addition to all the other animals, a large vulture in order to fulfill our every dream.

I returned home from school one, until then, lovely spring day to discover an aura of a chill normally only experienced in mid-winter. My mother's jaws were clenched to the degree that her attempts to hold a rational conversation were completely frustrated. To insulate himself from the spousal fury he had aroused, Daddy was into his fifth or sixth glass of straight bourbon, not that he ever really needed an excuse for that particular activity.

The cause of this little tempest was staked out in the backyard with a leather thong secured to one scaly leg, attached to a wooden peg driven into the turf. The damn bird was nearly as tall as I was and, fortunately for any thoughts I might have had for feminine companionship, a hell of a lot uglier than I was. Only years later did I realize that some life forms can be so awful to look at that they approach a beauty of their own. The vulture not only looked ugly, he smelled ugly. It wasn't long before I became convinced that he was ugly inside and out.

It's not going to come as any great surprise for me to tell you that I was assigned the responsibility of making this large, feathered gargoyle, a happy camper. To be quick about it, I failed. The bird and I immediately reached a reciprocal, intense dislike of each other and he had a distinct advantage over me. I was forbidden, on pain of getting my butt warmed, from the use of any form of force or physical coercion in attempting to discipline or domesticate the buzzard. He, on the other hand, was not burdened with any restraints of any sort, and utilized a whole arsenal of tricks in punishing me. He would, at every opportunity, belt me with his wings. If that didn't put me off he would use his beak which was like getting whacked with a ball hammer. Those devices were not his best shot. When he would determine that pummeling me, one way or another, was not sufficient to display his displeasure, he'd let me get close enough so that he could, *and would*, puke, whatever half-digested food he had in his craw, all over me. Now once, after stuffing herself with too much salmon for dinner, my sister had done that to me, and I didn't appreciate it. You bet that if I didn't cotton to my sister spraying me with her dinner, I sure as hell didn't warm up to having the bird barf all over me.

This particular tale has a happy ending. One morning, when the cause of all this misery, my father, went out to see his pet, he discovered a leather thong unattached to the critter. The old buzzard had flown the coop. Several days were spent by the family speculating as to just how the bird had managed to slip the tie from his leg. I realize that, at the time, I didn't know the benefits of the Fifth Amendment but, I sure as hell understood the virtue of not volunteering any opinion about the departure of the buzzard. My mother, who had an inherent suspicious nature, may have formed an opinion, but given her mind set regarding this addition to the family, which never changed from day one, she did not give voice to her deductions. I don't suppose that the opportunity to have a pet vulture is a common occurrence in anyone's life and fortunately, for all of us, my father only got one shot at it. Had there been a second acquisition of such a foul fowl, I'm' convinced my mother would have made him eat it.

Some years later, the last year and a half that I lived on the farm, I caught a young sparrow hawk, just out of the nest, and capable of flying only ten to fifteen feet at a launch. He couldn't fly too well, but he sure could bite. I had recalled reading somewhere, that you could tame a raptor by breathing tobacco smoke into its nostrils, so I decided to test this proposition. I lit a cigarette, placed a clean sock over his head, I actually had one, and blew in a mouthful of smoke into his beak. Damn if it didn't work. I had named him, for reasons that presently escape me, Junior. I kept him in my room, where he could fly around freely when not snoozing. I had a deer's head on one wall and Junior selected the antlers as his roost. At night time he would fly up to one of the horn tips, rustle around a little, preen his feathers, and eventually draw up one foot, settling down for the night.

One side of our house was covered with ivy and populated with a large flock of English sparrows. These poor birds became the main source of Junior's banquets. It's not something I would do to-day, but back then I had a much more callous approach to such matters and it seemed perfectly logical that a sparrow hawk should be fed sparrows. Junior, naturally, was in complete agreement with that menu and ate the little birds with much gusto.

I had not, and never did, clip his wings. Some sort of bonding had taken place and until I eventually turned him loose, he never tried to fly away. Junior was a travelling man, and enjoyed immensely rid-ing in my car. He would sit on the top of the passenger seat, walking back and forth as we drove along, occasionally chirping at some item of interest. Junior liked to be scratched on the back of his head and when he decided it was the proper time for such attention, he would perch on my shoulder and chew on my earlobes. It was sort of a 'hey, you scratch me and I'll scratch you.'

Sparrow hawks are truly one of nature's real beauties and Jun-ior was no exception. When he had his first, fully matured set of feathers, he was magnificent. The combination of his colors, red, blue, yellow, black and white, coupled with the striking way they were orchestrated, was a tribute to Mother Nature. She could give lessons to Michelangelo. A few years ago, my sister, whom I have come to appreciate as a warm human being rather than a pain in the ass, commissioned a water color of a male sparrow hawk, which she gave me. It is the spitting image of Junior and something I cherish.

Junior, unlike all of the other naturally wild creatures I ever at-tempted to tame, was both a good pet and a friend. He didn't really have any bad habits, at least none that I viewed as such. It is true that he wasn't exactly house trained and, as a result, the antlers on which he perched, as well as a substantial portion of the deer's head, were liberally white-washed with his droppings. To me this was not a major fault, however, the lady that was taking care of the house at that time, had a totally different perspective on the subject. She had the unreasonable opinion that policing up bird droppings didn't fit in her job description. Since, at the time, only my grandfather and I were still living at the farm, and neither of us could cook worth diddly, we were not in a position of strength to dispute her claims. As a result, with the ongoing build-up of droppings, the deer's head began to look like Mount Fuji.

At some point during our association, I discovered that Junior liked lean, beef hamburger and this, with an occasional, unlucky sparrow became his main source of provender. There was only one meal he liked better and, for the life of me, I do not remember how I discovered it. Anyway, what he liked most was hamburger, soaked in beer. I would roll the meat in little balls the size of a twenty-five cent piece and immerse it in a cup of beer. When presented with this delicacy, the little dipsomaniac would dance up and down, chortle, chirp and chomp. It would only take a couple of these gastronomic booze balls to make him falling down drunk, and sleepy. Once sated with the goodies, he would navigate his way to his perch, usually requiring a third or fourth effort, and attempt to roost. The problem he had was as soon as he would pull up one foot he would lose his balance and nearly fall off the horn. Since he was a bright bird, he naturally figured there was something wrong with his technique relating to his perching foot and he would reverse the procedure, next time drawing up the opposite foot, with the same result. Ultimately, he would compromise and settle down, using both feet to hang onto what must have seemed to him to be a roost in a wild, wind storm. I had one of my best friends staying with us at the time. He had, at the end of World War II, just been discharged from the Marines. We'd be mellowing out on our own beers and, watching our mutually inebriated friend, go into hysterical laughter.

In the late winter of 1947, a university in Colorado had accepted my application as a candidate for a degree of higher learning. This was an event for which I, and all of my family, were very grateful. Given the number of rejections from eastern universities who had, no doubt, keener judgment of the suitability of my groping for further education, anything short of reform school was accepted as a triumph.

It was necessary to return Junior to the wild. I put him outside and weaned him from the little balls of alcoholic beef. The strange thing was that almost immediately his mother showed up and for over two weeks they sat, side by side, on the telephone lines that serviced the house. The last sight I had of my little friend, as I drove away from home, to go into town and commence my journey to the west, was of Junior, with his mother flying along with him, following the car for about two miles until, finally, they both perched on a fence line where, as I disappeared, I am sure his mother was giving him instructions right out of a temperance pamphlet.

My final experience in domesticating a wild creature occurred many years later. By then, contrary to all of the well-considered opin-

ions of my relatives to the contrary, I had actually been awarded a degree from an accredited university and had married a city girl. The lady who made that choice was truly a city person. One example that certifies the truth of that statement is that, shortly after our wedding, we were driving down a narrow, two-lane road in Iowa and were caught behind a bright, green farm tractor that had, written across its rear-end, the name of John Deere. My lady, seeing this, exclaimed, "Oh look, isn't' that cute! He's got his name on the back." Enough said.

I had graduated from the university and we were living in New Haven, Connecticut, where I had a job, for the summer, working on an agricultural, experimental farm. Into my arms came a cute, little, fuzzy skunk that I took to a local veterinarian to excise his stinker.

We named him Petite Putoi, Pootie for short. We had this belief, or at least I did, because the city girl couldn't have known one way or the other, that Pootie could be just like a cat as a pet. Well, let me tell you, it just ain't so. This little rascal was not like a cat the day he was born, nor was he, the day he died. He was, and remained, essentially a wild animal. He became a good, if not troublesome friend, but never a pet.

Skunks are mainly nocturnal animals, so for the most part he would sleep soundly all day long and, then when we were ready to settle down for the night, Pootie would emerge, bright-eyed and bushy tailed, to start his day. His day was to get into every bit of mischief he could dream of.

He had very powerful front paws and easily opened cabinet doors, closet doors, or virtually anything that caught his curiosity, and he had an immense curiosity.

Early on, he developed an intense fascination for the garbage can and, if given the opportunity, would spread its contents all over the kitchen floor. To put an end to this particular recreation, we had to chain the cabinet doors closed.

This black and white striped critter had a very broad range in his dinner desires. A gourmet he was not. The meal he liked best was baked beans, with Russian salad dressing, topped with chocolate sauce. Ugh!

Early on we introduced him to the idea of personal hygiene, i.e. potty training, and provided him with the latest, state-of-the-art kitty, litter box. Pootie was a very intelligent little devil and he quickly grasped the fundamentals of toilet training. The problem was that he could be and often was a perverse little bastard. After several weeks of religiously performing properly within his litter box, he would walk up to it, kick it across the floor and crap on the rug.

Mother Nature gave skunks teeth that are a cross between a surgeon's scalpel and narrow, pointed daggers. They are not their primary defense system, being mainly for eating meat. Nevertheless, their choppers are lethal weapons. Pootie could be, and often was, a very affectionate animal. He would often hop up on the couch where I was seated, stretch out, and enjoy being scratched behind the ears, or stroked like a cat. To show his appreciation for such treatment he would, in turn, munch on the hairs on the back of my forearms. It was sort of like eating corn on the cob, a meal that he liked very much, or perhaps he was grooming me for fleas. The problem was that his temperament was mercurial to say the least and, he would go from being affectionate to downright vicious in a split second. In his manic moods, he would sink his fangs in the most readily accessible portion of my arm he could chomp upon. He didn't just bite and let go. He would clamp down with powerful jaws and then shake his head from side to side. The result would be a damn severe laceration. The only way I found to stop this destructive pest from sending me to the emergency ward was to immediately grasp him by the nape of his neck, twist him loose, and toss him on the floor, at which point he would stomp off highly angry.

Skunks, and Pootie was no exception, are cute as hell. The immediate impulse, on seeing one in a domestic setting, is to stick out a finger to play cootchie-cootchie. When friends would visit, and make our little friend's acquaintance for the first time, we would warn them not to do this. That was just like putting up a 'wet paint' sign and the result was as predictable as night follows day. Pootie would, being presented with a digital member, bite, and we would be into the medicine cabinet to render first aid.

A skunk's first line of defense is the ability to spray anything it perceives as a threat with a very obnoxious, liquid material, the smell of which is beyond description. It's an interesting fact that dogs never learn to leave skunks alone. Dogs have the same belief, in their ultimate ability to triumph over porcupines, as they do over skunks and it is a mistake. They will, with dedication, get pissed on, or quilled, again and again. Dogs must have this dream of a heaven where over these two adversaries, they will always come out the winner.

Pootie, of course, had his shooter removed. That didn't prevent his attempting to use it. Given the chance, before a skunk sprays, he will stamp his feet, as a warning. If that doesn't convince you that he's about to get it on, he'll turn his body so that he can bore-sight you with both ends, at which point in time, wisdom dictates that you back off, rapidly. With Pootie, reduced to rage, he would aim at you and strain mightily to blast you with his non-existent squirter.

The best he could produce were little bursts of flatulence, after which he would sulk, stiff-legged into a closet.

Pootie was the first pet my bride and I had and, notwithstanding his fits of temper, we were very attached to this furry friend. We spoiled him rotten. He was overweight and, because our quarters were air-conditioned, his fur coat was very thick. On our way from the East Coast, to the West, while travelling through the mountains in West Virginia in the middle of the summer, Pootie died from heat and excitement. We stopped by the side of the road and buried him. He went down wet.

Pootie

Chapter 6: Snips and Snails and Puppy-Dog Tails

There have been only a few brief periods of my life when I didn't have at least one dog. These intelligent friends truly deserve their characterization as 'Man's best friend.' They will return mistreatment with love and loyalty and over the years I've become aware of some exceptionally terrible situations involving the abuse of dogs by their masters but invariably the animal, once having committed, remains attached to its' tormentor.

On a farm, dogs are a must. They can be taught all sorts of useful things. At least most of them can. Our canine population was never less than three and at times, not counting puppies, was as high as seven. All were inside, outside dogs. During the summer they generally slept on our front porch. This was actually a long veranda, stretching sixty to seventy feet across the front of the house with a width of twenty feet or so. On a summer's evening, during the times we had a full population of mutts, the veranda would look like an immense fur rug with all of our dogs sprawled out in a comic variety of positions, grunting, snoring or yelping.

For the most part they got along well with each other. They played and wrestled around, chased cats for fun, and joined each other in a howling chorus to greet any strange visitors. Most were mutts of an undetermined pedigree. Over the period of my first seventeen years, we had so many I cannot now do fairness to all of them. I do, however, recall a few real stand-outs.

One of the few pedigreed dogs we had was a pure-bred Great Dane, named Gunnar. Gunny for short, (pronounced Gooney). Actually he was my mother's dog and while he was protective of the whole family, he was fiercely attached to my mother, also known as 'Miss Betty.' Gunny was a dark charcoal in color and very big. He must have stood a good three feet flat-footed and when he would rear up to greet me, he easily knocked me flat. He also out-weighed me by a bunch of pounds. Gunny had a long tail that was hooked up to some perpetual motion muscle in his butt. He'd come into the house, bound around with his floppy old ears flying and his tail wagging like a black snake whip. One trip around the living room would result in everything placed on the tables being swept onto the floor. Of all of our dogs, Gunny was just about the dumbest one we ever had. It's a miracle that he eventually did become house-trained and that didn't exactly happen overnight. My mother never was able to break him of the habit of cleaning off the tables.

His concern for the safety of 'Miss Betty' was monumental. Normally he was just a big, dumb, happy-go-lucky slob but, any perceived threat to my mother would turn him into a Viking berserker. I remember a visit we had from some old school girl buddy of my mother's. They hadn't seen each other for years and you know how that goes. This lady, was damn near six feet tall and horsey. The way she was set up she could have carried the horse. Anyway, the lady came bounding out of her car and up on to the porch, at which point, both she and my mother commenced squealing and shrieking at each other the way women do, and rushed into each other's arms. Gunny immediately perceived this as an attack upon 'Miss Betty' by a raving Amazon, and he went into action immediately. Since the lady was hugging my mother, he went for the best shot he could get and bit her on the right cheek of her rear-end. I mean he bit her good. She had a full set of canine denture holes, top and bottom, and Gunny wasn't disposed to let go of the ham. My father finally persuaded him that there was no need for such heroic activity and separated Gunny from the old friend whose shrieks, by now, had taken on a whole different quality. You could have heard her through three counties. I wouldn't have believed she could make more noise. She proved me wrong when my mother got her into the upstairs bathroom and began swabbing her rear with iodine. Whooeee!

As a family we generally ate our evening meal together in our dining room, with 'Miss Betty' at one end of a long walnut dining table and my grandfather at the other. During mealtimes that was the only room that the dogs were forbidden to enter. Gunny never grasped the reason for this exclusion but he made us pay dearly. He would sit, in the doorway between the living room and the dining room, with a woebegone mournful pair of eyes. What was causing his grief was seeing all the deliciously smelling goodies going around the table. As he sat, and sniffed, his salivary glands would go into high gear and he would begin to drool. Pretty soon we'd have this big slob sitting there with two steady streams of spit running out of each side of his mouth onto the floor where he would create a pool you could swim in. You talk about an appetizing sight. One view of this act could put you on a hunger strike. Back then I wasn't exactly a big eater and, much to 'Miss Betty's irritation I frequently dawdled through a meal, especially if it was something I didn't like, such as salmon. I learned to blame it all on Gunny which really put her in a bind.

We had a lot of cats: both house cats and barn cats. They are an absolute necessity on a farm. The dogs, and especially Gunny, liked to chase them. They never chewed them up, just the chase was a fun thing to do. Especially since the cats, not being absolutely certain that it was play time, would normally run like hell to get away from their tormentors. However, we had one really mean, non-descript lady cat who wouldn't put up with any nonsense and who had a strong aversion to having her tranquility interrupted by the woof brigade. To Gunny, all cats looked the same and he was never able to distinguish one from another. All of our other dogs gave miss puss a wide berth, but not old slobbers. He made a very bad judgment call one day when he decided he wanted to chase the lady at a time when she was raising a litter of kittens. His invitation to play was rejected out-of-hand. The little mother, who was maybe one-fiftieth of his size, in one leap, flew onto his shoulders where she fastened her front claws securely in his hide and started spurring him with her hind paws, each of which was equipped with five sabers. That dog took off on a dead run with miss puss raking him at every leap. She looked like a bare-back bronc rider and she sure as hell met the ten second bell.

At one time or another all of our dogs, in their respective younger days, took a fancy to a little chicken dinner. This was a big crime and, on a farm like ours, was right up there with sheep killing. It was, however, a matter that if treated immediately and severely, would be prevented from becoming a habit. My grandfather 'Pop' had the cure. As soon as one of our friends made its first kill that we could discover, the chicken carcass would be tied by its hind legs with baling twine tightly under the mutt's chin, where the chicken could not be gotten to, and where it would hang until it rotted. Naturally, the sentenced felon was persona non grata in the house during the course of treatment. It usually took about three weeks for the putrid bird to finally reach a state of decomposition that would separate it from the dog. You can understand that carrying a bib like that around for a couple of weeks would dampen your desire for a little filet of fowl.

In our area we had a large population of skunks. I mentioned earlier that, for reasons I never learned, dogs never get tired of taking them on. The results were always the same skunk - one, dog - zero. This includes the smartest dogs we had. I don't believe there was a single encounter between one of our friends and a wood-pussy that the friend won. It's for sure we never saw any dead skunks and we sure got to clean up a lot of very smelly dogs. If it was during the more sublime months we'd just let them stay outside until the perfume faded away. In the winter they would get a bath in tomato juice, which really worked. That's to say it got rid of the smell until the next time and there always was a 'next time.' I suspect that a dog's idea of heaven is a place where they always triumph over these little stripped squirters.

One of the best natured dogs we ever had was mostly Spitz, with something else mixed in. He was pure white, with a dense furry coat. Exercising great imagination my sister and I agreed to name him Cotton. 'Miss Betty,' who had a flair for descriptive phrases, re-ferred to him as "The dog with a lavender soul." He was very intelligent, leaving aside the business with skunks, and very affection-ate. Cotton was the best dog we had for herding anything. He just simply liked it and when put to work, brought in the cows from pas-ture, rounded up the horses and the goats. He was such a nice fellow that none of the animals were spooked by him. He like herding things so much he would practice on baby chicks, cats, ducks, geese, you name it, with the exception of miss puss. Unlike Gunny, Cotton had great respect for her view of dogs. He left her alone and she recipro-cated.

Cotton had one major problem. He truly believed that he was the greatest lover since Errol Flynn. Everybody loved Cotton, includ-ing the lady dogs. Well, not quite everybody, all of the time. During those periods when one of the ladies would indicate a readiness for a little hot romancing, none of the male dogs liked each other. Unfortunately, for lover boy, Cotton was not the biggest dog on the farm. The biggest dog was Gunny. They got cross-wise with each other over a non-descript bitch mutt who obviously appeared to each of them as a reincarnation of Helen of Troy. With raging hormones Cotton thought he was Genghis Kahn, and he threw down his gauntlets at Gunny's feet, prepared to do battle for the fair maid. At half the size, and maybe one-third the weight of his chosen adversary, it was not a good judgment call. It was like matching Willie Pep against Joe Louis. Cotton's libido was probably bigger than Gunny's, it's just the rest of him was not. What was really a tragic comedy was that the lady in question was smaller than both of them and, as it pertained to Gunny, was so much smaller he couldn't connect with her anyway, while Cotton could have, given the chance. I say could have because the fight, one-sided as it was, between the two of them, must have started a half-hour or so before I got home. What I saw was, by then, a crimson Spitz being mauled by a very angry dog. The only reason Cotton wasn't dead is that he had that marvelous thick fur rug all over his body and, as a result, mostly what Gunny got was a mouthful of fluff. The density of the ruff around Cotton's jugular saved his life. Even so, he was one, whipped puppy. By the time Cotton had recuperated from the mauling Gunny had inflicted upon him, the object of their mutual affection was no longer stimulating anyone to mortal combat. The whole affair didn't turn into an Arthurian fable where staunch knight wins fair lady. Looking back, my perception of the whole event is that little boy dogs are not that much different from little boy humans when it comes to fair ladies.

I have some more canine friends to talk about but the last that stick in my mind, before I left the farm, were two collies who were sisters from the same litter. One was mine and one was my sisters. Mine, named Crickett, was mostly a golden yellow, with a magnificent ruff, a snow, white vest and dainty white paws. Her sister, Heather, was a tri-color, predominantly black and white, with brown eyebrows. The only problem with these ladies, and they indeed were ladies, is that they were not overly endowed with brains. They had, as most collies do today, long, narrow skulls that limited their brain

space. This is the result of years of selective breeding for show pur-
poses that produced elegant looking animals, sacrificing non-visible
characteristics. It's not a new story, and is one that has been repeated
again, and again, as any particular breed has reached a level of popu-
larity. A combination of in-breeding and narrowly perceived
selection has not necessarily benefited man's best friends. Bright, or
smart, Crickett and Heather were really great friends. I don't have any
especially interesting anecdotes to tell about either, it's just that, in
Crickett's case she was the last canine friend that I had before leaving
the farm, and I had her for about four years. On week-ends, when I
would be rambling around the area, she would accompany me. She
radiated exuberance. She could dance on air, always gay, affectionate
and obedient. She was to me Lassie, only she really was, and he really wasn't. I swear this dog could talk. She had a smile that could
have sold toothpaste. Now that I think about it, she never chased a
skunk. She was so fastidious that the smell would have appalled her.
She had a particularly endearing way of showing affection. If I were
sitting down, she'd come up, place her head in my lap, wag her bushy
tail, and growl softly, looking up with smiling eyes. I have to tell you
that those eyes on a female human would have been eyes to die for.

When I left the farm, to go to college in Colorado, I could not
take Crickett with me, so I left her with Pop. I didn't regret leaving
the farm but parting with that lady was a hard, hard day and a wet
one. Pop was, by that time, over the hill and just not up to keeping
the farm running. He was the only one left. Mouse had moved to
Connecticut with our maternal grandmother. 'Miss Betty,' some years
after my father's death, had remarried and moved to New York and I
had gone west. As a result, the farm was sold and Crickett went to the
local humane society. I regret that to this day and no friend was ever
so badly served.

- - - - - - - - - - - -- - - - - - - - - - -- - - - - - - - - - - - - - - - - - -- - - - - - - - - - -- -

"Sugar and spice and everything nice,
That's what little girls are made of. *
Snips and snails and puppy dogs tails
That's what little boys are made of."

* The exception is a teen-aged, older sister.

Chapter 7: The French Connection

A gap occurred in my life during which I didn't have any friends. This was the result of going away to college and the early years in the Marine Corps. After our marriage, the first pet my wife and I had was Pootie. We had gotten into tropical fish at one point, but they didn't really qualify as friends. Fish were more a curiosity item, not being something you could cuddle up to.

Having buried Pootie in the mountains of West Virginia, we proceeded west to Camp Pendleton where we rented a house on the base. I was given an artillery battery assignment which, for most of the time, was an eight to five job, and allowed me to be around the house on a civilized schedule.

I came home one evening and was greeted by the 'City Girl' with a wondrous tale of her having found the absolute dream puppy at a pet store in Oceanside. Having been without a friend for some time I was, naturally, vulnerable to her suggestion that we really needed to have a dog. However, in the circuitous route she had learned to follow when conning me into something that she anticipated I might initially reject, she didn't jump right out at first and tell me what type of dog she had seen. She is an artist at the slow wind up, followed by the fast curve. "A French poodle? You've got to be crazy. I'm a Marine. All of my friends are going to think I've turned queer." What I had in mind, as a more appropriate friend, was a big, burly dog, like a Doberman or a German Shepherd. Certainly not some little foo foo puppy.

With the innate wisdom, and guile, that all female critters are born with, my wife didn't push the subject. She would have made a natural fly fishing expert. She's very adept at tossing a little bait out with the certain knowledge that, with a little patience, the fish will always bite, sooner or later.

About a week after her initial sortie, we went into town for a little shopping and on our way home, Machiavelli suggested we look in at the pet store to see what types of puppies they had. Understand that she knew what kind of puppies they had. One kind. Poodles. Anyway, the suggestion seemed a reasonable one to me and since my wife had not been put off with my rejection of the concept of a Marine housing some French poof, I felt it only fair to accept her thought, so in we went. What they had was a litter of black, miniature French poodles. One of those little suckers had a "take me home" look from nose to tail. I mean that puppy was "Mr. Personality." No reasonable person is going to resist petting any puppy and certainly not any of the ones in that store. You can predict the end result. In less time than it takes to write this, we were on the way home with a black, male, miniature French poodle. All of my virile, macho comments regarding owning such a dog were gone. We named him Pretty Pierre, called Pete for short. As things turned out, Pete is right up there as one of the three best dogs I've ever known. I do not believe there are dogs with more natural intelligence than poodles. Certainly not any I've ever known.

Having overcome my unfounded objections to owning a poodle, and with some thought to the expense of Pete's purchase, it came to me that what we should do was buy a female. That way we could produce our own puppies, sell them at the outrageous price we had paid for Pete, and get our money back. My bride and I hadn't been married long enough for her to have learned that not all of my brilliantly planned economic schemes would pan out. I can't say that she jumped right out in accepting my suggestion but, on the other hand, she didn't veto it. As a result, we acquired a second miniature, French poodle. She was a silver/grey and we named her Desiree, Dede for short. She was every bit as cute, and smart, as was Pete and, as it turned out, maybe even smarter. That may not be an accurate judgment. It's just that, typically female, she was more devious.

With Pete and Dede onboard I figured it was just a matter of time until they got old enough to commence presenting us with a crop of our own. It didn't turn out that way. Dede just never seemed to

take romance to heart. Somewhere along the line that part of her French-ness was left out. Pete certainly ap-peared to be a role model of froggy manliness but Dede could have easily qualified for a nun-nery. On one occasion, we even enticed her with cookies, in an at-tempt to get her to stand still long enough to enable Pete to effect a passionate union. Dede was a true cookie hound and nothing, other than a tasty lamb bone, so consumed her attention, than a chocolate chip. It didn't work. In time she be-came known as the "Iron Maiden." Naturally, this was all very frustrating to me and, in addition, not exactly a paying proposition. It did, however, occur to me that the solution was to acquire a second female- the theory being that Dede was a mischance and that with a truly hot little-girl poodle we could still re-coup our investment. I think by now the City Girl had some real reservations. However, hav-ing been the instigator of the French collection she wasn't in any position from which she could take a firm stand and object, so we got the third dog. She was apricot in color and we hopefully named her "Sukin Sin", which translated means "little bitch"- calling her Suki for short. Suki was, like my other two, non-productive friends, very smart. She was all female and when she matured, a true French lady. Given the right times of the year, she could draw little boy dogs through reinforced concrete. Did we get puppies? Hell no. It turned out the old macho Pete didn't have any lead in his pencil. At that point it also occurred to us that maybe there really wasn't anything funny about Dede, but that what it could be was that all along she was

aware of Pete's empty pistol and just didn't want to waste time with a blank shooter. Anyway, with three dogs and no puppies, I finally reached the conclusion that maybe this just wasn't the type of home venture for us and we didn't acquire any new pups. We did, however, enjoy many years with the three we had. Each, in their own way, was a distinct individual. All were smart as hell, tremendously affectionate, and people persons. Pete had a real sense of humor and enjoyed playing tricks on my wife. One of his favorite games would be to sneak into the kitchen, or pantry, grab her dish towel and run under a table with it, waiting for her to take it back. She would grab one end while Pete held on to the other, growling fiercely. He wouldn't let loose whereupon, invariably reaching an upper level of indignation, the 'City Girl' would shout at him, "Let go you son-of-a-bitch." One night, when our daughter was about three years old I had, upon coming home, picked her up and was holding her upside down, at which point she squawked, "Let me go you son bitch." Well we know where she got that language.

All three dogs liked cashew nuts, Pete in particular. He could be taught, quickly, just about anything, when offered a cashew as a reward. He learned to sit, lie down and roll over during about a half hours' training session. He liked to please. All of these pups were good with our children and very much aware that they were a part of the family. Among the three of them, Pete was the alpha member and, in typical French macho style, he would always insist that the ladies respect his manly right to first place. If a nice soft, lamb bone was available Pete would bully the two girls and take the first shot at chewing it up and, in most cases that meant all of it. This was a serious matter to Dede because she like the marrow better than cashews.

One evening she figured out a solution to Pete's arbitrary choice of ownership over the bone. As was his usual way, Pete had taken possession of an exceptionally nice bone and was under the dining room table where he began to savor it and, at the same time, glaring slantwise at Dede, who made it plain to him she wanted the bone. Any gentlemen would have at least let her have a couple of licks but not our little frog. What Dede did was ingenious. She ran to the back door, where Pete couldn't see her from the dining room, and began to bark the way she would if a stranger was at the door. This, of course, aroused Pete's protective instincts for the sanctity of the home and, like a true knight, he left his bone, and roared to the defense. After all it was the alpha dog's primary responsibility to protect hearth and home and, the idea that a mere slip of a girl was taking over his prerogatives, was something not to be tolerated. Dede, as soon as she knew she had suckered him away from the bone, ran around him as he rushed to the back door, grabbed the bone, and disappeared under the living room couch where Pete just couldn't get at her. Mad? Boy was he mad. You can't tell me dogs can't cuss because that one could and did. A Marine drill sergeant could have taken lessons from the things he said to Dede, who couldn't have cared less. She had the bone and kept it.

Pete neither forgot Dede's deception nor forgave her and from that point on, we began to have problems with the dogs. Pete and Suki were both smaller than Dede but they ganged up on her given the least excuse and we would have some nasty fights as a result. The worst one occurred during an evening when my wife and I had gone out to dine, leaving an elderly couple baby-sitting the kids. Not knowing the latent animosity that had developed among our three friends, they put some scraps down as a treat for the dogs. Pete, with Suki assisting, got into it with Dede and she was taking a beating. Our baby-sitters got Pete isolated from Dede and that's all she needed. Dede turned on Suki and damn near killed her. We got a call at the restaurant and rushed home. The living room looked like a slaughter house with blood all over the walls. Little Suki was nearly bled dry and we were just able to get her to a vet in time. Following that fracas, we started a policy of putting Dede in a separate room for safety whenever we were going to be out of the house.

All My Friends

I can only recall one other major fight that the three of them got into and it was a riot. Our daughter talked us into getting a flocked tree for Christmas, something we had never done before and sure as hell haven't done since. We always put the presents under our Christmas tree and, unfortunately, one present given us by relatives included chocolate candies as a part of the wrapping. Our three friends, each of whom, had a nose like a homing radar, very quickly sniffed out the goodies. Virtually simultaneously, they dove under the flocked bush to gobble them up. There was no taking sides on this one, it was every dog for itself. The war that resulted, tipped over the tree and, by the time these hounds from hell got through thrashing around, they had white fluff all over the room and our daughter was in tears over the destruction of her tree.

Prior to the acquisition of Suki, when we just had Pete and Dede, I was sent to Fort Sill, near Lawton, Oklahoma, to attend an artillery school run by the Army. We took the pups with us. At the time, they were loaded with fleas. When we returned to California about four months later, neither dog had a single flea. Even fleas couldn't survive in that part of the country, at least California fleas couldn't. That's the only part of the country where you can be ankle deep in dust and butt deep in mud at one and the same time. In Lawton they called French poodles "eyetraillion" dogs for reasons that escaped us. I guess maybe they didn't see too many poodles in that part of the country, being more partial to mixed varieties of hounds.

Pete and Dede, prior to the bone trick and before Suki's arrival, got along well together. Looking back, I think it was a mistake to have three dogs in the same house. Anyway, one of their favorite games was playing tug of war with a chain of old socks tied together. This sport was always accompanied with blood thirsty growls and snarls. Dede usually had the advantage as the heavier of the two but Pete being more tenacious was not always the loser. When Dede won getting the prize away from Pete, she would dart under the couch as she later did with the bone. Pete, on the occasions when he triumphed, would prance around the house tossing the socks in the air.

Of the three, Dede was the sweetest. She would always welcome me home with a big grin and, like cricket, was truly an ipana model. She used her smile to get cookies and her success ratio was phenomenal. When our first born was still in the ankle-biting stage we kept her under control in a crib. The surrounding area was pretty

much undeveloped and had a large population of rattlesnakes. It was Dede's frantic barking that alerted my wife that a rattler was about to join our daughter in her pen. At the time we were naturally concerned for her safety. Upon further consideration, I now believe that snake wouldn't have had a snowball's chance in Hell.

Suki and Dede were the first of the three to pass on to the big fireplug in the sky. Their going was deeply lamented by all of us, but we still had Pete, who had reached senior citizen status and for all of his ornery tricks, held a spot in my heart few of my friends ever achieved.

The 'City Girl' had acquired a large Desert Afghan who you'll meet further down the road. He was easily ten times Pete's size. She named him Kushka but, due to the weird way he barked, he got the nickname of Oofy. He was a very gentle dog and, notwithstanding his substantial size advantage over Pete, he gave the Frenchman all the respect due his senior years and his status as the premier dog. Pete, on his part, welcomed having the big mutt. I think he missed the two ladies.

My wife used to walk Oofy on a leash at night and Pete, free running, would accompany them. He was, as a result of age, developing cataracts in his eyes. One evening, not seeing a neighbor's car rounding a curve in the road, Pete ran in front and was hit. I rushed him to our local vet but the damage was too severe and the recommendation was to put him down, painlessly, and I assented.

All My Friends

When it was over, I brought Pete home, chose a choice spot, and buried him. It was a bad night and I ended up very drunk, lost in an impenetrable orange grove fifty feet from the house.

Lisa and Pete

Lisa and Suki

Chapter 8: Pussies of Many Colors

From my earliest memories, I recall a long line of cats. I've written about our rodeo queen who took our stupid Dane for a fast gallop. On the farm she was but one of many.

At some point, I got my own personal cat. He was a black Tom with a bobbed tail, named Loki. The short tail was genetic, and he passed it on to his children, that is those that were black. Winters, in that part of the country, could get very cold and the strongest memory I have of Loki is his crawling under my bed sheets, curling around my toes and going to sleep. It was better than a hot water bottle. Tom cats, to the uninitiated, appear lazy. They spend an awful lot of time seeking nice, warm, comfortable places to get in some serious snoozing. Once in a while they'll do a little hunting but, that is not as serious an enterprise as it is with lady cats, especially those with kittens. The thing is the toms are not really lazy. They have sense enough to know that they must husband their energies in order to be able to perform their primary mission in life. That chore is to fight as many other toms as chance will afford them and to impregnate the greatest number of females. This type of arduous activity requires a lot of rest. Anyone that's ever heard a pair of mating cats can tell you that that is a high action event, taking lots of energy, and from all the noise that results, you can tell it's taken very seriously.

Most of our toms, Loki included, were battle scarred veterans, and in the waning days of his life his ears, more and more, began to look like shredded velvet. It's probably a good thing he had a bobbed tail because I'm sure that he would have lost most of a regular swisher in the wars. One big problem with toms is that their fights produce nasty puncture wounds that easily abscess. As a result, Loki was constantly in need of medical services.

After leaving the farm, I didn't have any cat friends until I left the Marines and settled, about thirty-four years ago, in our present home. This gap was closed when we were adopted by Big Daddy. Not too long after we moved into our home, my wife began to feed this huge, non-descript tom who had made it a regular habit to panhandle through the neighborhood. Apparently, having tested the various possibilities, he decided that we were the winners, and offered the best in gourmet foods and comfort. He knew he'd be fed twice a day and in between snacks he would curl up on the back porch and catch a few Z's.

I had never seen a cat as big as he was and I haven't seen once since. He had a head twice the size of most large toms, shoulders like a buffalo, and paws that could have doubled for bearpaw snow shoes.

Big Daddy got us back into the cat business in a big way. What happened, is that after deciding we were his type of suckers, he began to fetch his girlfriends and brought them home as permanent guests. Smart cat. It obviously occurred to him that he was expending too much time and precious energy roaming around for miles just to perform his tomly duties. What better solution than to stash his harem at home base. Whatever he had, he had a lot of it, because he had one hell of a lot of girlfriends, and we ended up with one hell of a lot of kittens.

One good by-product of all of this was a marked decrease in rats, mice and, believe it, rattlesnakes around the house. With the number of hard hunting ladies we had, anything catchable was in real jeopardy. Unfortunately, this included song birds, rabbits and quail. The 'City Girl' has a queer thing about quail and it caused her great remorse when one of our friends had a little tasty dinner of quail.

Big Daddy had more than his share of fights and, consequently, visits with the vet. His ears were shredded and he had more scars than a pro-hockey player. One thing is certain: to the day he died, he won his fights. No other tom ever took one of his ladies away from him, nor did any ever move in on his turf. Big Daddy went quietly to sleep on the back porch after a long active life. If I had been blessed with his libido, I would have syndicated it and put it on the market.

Among the grieving widows that Big Daddy left us with, were some calico ladies of great charm and beauty. Two in particular were standouts.

One of these was named Split Kitty. It was as if a ruler had been placed length-wise from her nose to her tail. One side was painted totally different from the other. It looked like someone had cemented the halves from two separate cats together.

A lot of people don't like cats. They often do not appear as friendly, loyal or affectionate as most dogs. They can be very independent and decide when they want to be rubbed, tickled or show any warmth. Split Kitty gave me indisputable proof of her trust in me. I was stretched out on our couch, on my back, watching TV one evening when that very pregnant lady sashayed into the house, jumped onto my belly and promptly began using me as a maternity ward. She had the whole damn litter right on me, mess and all. Now, I ask you, what's a feller' to do? What you do is squawk like hell for your wife to come rescue you. Women know about these things, most men sure as hell don't.

Our population of cat friends over the last thirty years or so has ebbed and flowed. Regretfully some have been lunched upon by coyotes and some have been enticed to locate elsewhere by neighboring toms, something that just never happened when Big Daddy was around. Related to Split Kitty was one of the prettiest calicos I've ever seen and she became our daughter's personal kitten virtually from birth. For reasons that may be genetic, the women in my family consistently come up with weird names for most of their pets and  this cat was called Tickalous Tiger- Tiki for short. She was unusual in that she bonded closely with my daughter and the two of them viewed each other with much warmth, a phenomenon a little unusual for a cat.

Tiki developed a calcium deficiency disorder, or something like that, that resulted in massive, suppurating sores on her hind legs. These would open up, clear down to the bone. Along with prescribed medicines, we treated her with hot soaks in Epsom salt solutions, and massage, but notwithstanding our best efforts, one of her hind legs atrophied and mummified from the knee down. Our vet recommended

that she be put to
sleep. My daughter
would not permit it,
saying that if Tiki
could talk she would
ask for a chance to
live. We went with
her and she was right.
Between my wife and
daughter they brought Tiki through the disease and nursed her back to
health. She did lose the lower part of her leg, which did not disad-
vantage her to any great degree. Tiki had always stuck pretty close
around the house so that she was reasonably safe from attack, and on
three legs she was still very agile. I have been very glad that we followed my brat's wishes. She really loved that cat and was at an age
where following our vet's advice might have caused a lasting hurt. As
it turned out the two had more years of joy with each other, as did the
rest of the family.

Almost all calico cats are female. The males, carrying these
genes, are usually yellow. Once in a great, great while, a male with
calico markings, will surface. These, at least those I've known, are
gay. The color, as I understand it, is a sex-linked characteristic, producing female pussies of many colors and burly, big yellow toms.

Somewhere along the line we reached a point where we were
out of cats. One reason is that our son was allergic to them and, as a
result, when the cat population wound down to zero we did not seek
replacements. After our children grew up, married, and more or less
left the family nest, we got back into the calico cat business.

My daughter brought us, a few years ago, a very pretty calico
lady who, after a reasonable period, decided we might be all right so
she decided to stick around. Having settled her housing business, she
made the next logical decision to beget. Her first litter, all calico ladies and yellow toms, did not survive birth by a week. We never
knew what caused this and were delighted when her second effort was
a major success. She delivered three toms and two ladies, all healthy
and all the right colors. However, she had six toes on her front paws
and so did two of her sons. One of these had paws so big they looked

like a catcher's mitt and he was named Johnny Bench. I wasn't able to persuade the 'City Girl' that we needed to keep all five of the kittens but, with some reluctance, she agreed to one male and one female, and these we have today.

The female was the prettier of the two, and the male, being the first born, was the biggest of the litter. The other three went to homes of friends.

Possum, the female, has developed into a very independent person. She comes for meals when she damn well chooses. She will seek a little petting when, and if, it pleases her. The rest of the time she walks to the beat of her own drum and, strangely, cannot tolerate her big brother. Whenever he tries to remind her of the fun they had playing as kittens, she responds with nastiest hissing and spitting I've ever heard.

Duke, the tom, named after a famous actor, is a great cat. He comes when he's called, like a dog. He is always ready for a little wrestling or rubbing and has a purr motor that can go into high gear instantly. He's big, although not close to Big Daddy, and unusual for a tom, does a journeyman's job in the rate and mouse department.

Around our patio we have a bunch of ponds where we grow water lilies, koi, and goldfish. Duke is fascinated by the fish. One of his favorite meals is a trout dinner sold by Whiskas. He can often be found crouched down by the edge of a pond, watching the fish, swishing his very bushy tail, and obviously contemplating the delight of a little fresh dinner. He has one major problem that prevents him realizing such delights. He hates water. Now almost every cat I've ever known did not take kindly to water but, with Duke, the dislike goes to the pathological. The only way he could get a fish would be to dip a paw in the pond and snag one. That would require getting it wet, and that's something unthinkable. His phobia regarding moisture is such that a light fog at night will drive him indoors and, God forbid it should rain. When it does, he's in for the duration.

One Sunday, our son stopped by for a little burnt meat, which is to say I was cooking on the bar-b-que. Duke had his two front paws on the edge of one of the ponds, with his nose about a half an inch above the water, drooling over a little fillet of fish. The rest of him, including his hind feet were on the concrete, patio slab. Duke's concentration over a possible fin dinner was so great I doubt if he even knew anyone else was on the patio. My son snuck up behind him and goosed him in the butt. Completely startled, Duke arched up on his hind legs and launched himself over the pond when he realized he was in deep trouble. In a desperate attempt to avoid going in the tank, and with a terrified yowl, he dug his hind claws into the cement and lunged for the far side. He did not make it but he did leave two sets of parallel claw marks gouged into the cement. They look like they were scribed with a cold chisel. Duke ended up, with a belly flop, in the pond. He came out of there faster than he went in and he was one wet, mad cat. I don't believe he has forgiven my son for his prank, and I know he hasn't forgotten it. He still stalks the ponds but he never turns his back on anyone.

Cats are not really loquacious. They'll howl to come in, yowl to go out and holler for their dinner. Duke is a talker. When he marches into the house he starts squawking half a block away. He'll lie on the couch and meow, purr, squawk and talk. He follows me out to

the corrals and talks all the way out and back. I haven't got his accent totally worked out but generally he's just telling us that he's a happy camper.

Big Daddy was in a special class all by himself and I don't expect I'll come across another quite like him. The pussies of many colors have been, and are a source of much enjoyment. I anticipate many years with Duke and Possum. I expect she'll just get more bitchy and Duke will never grow up.

Chapter 9: Feathers and Fins

Bringing home a wild buzzard was not my father's sole venture into exotic birds. Prior to the Roosevelt-Landon presidential campaign, he brought us two parrots. One was a Mexican yellow head and the other a Mexican green head. The yellow head was a magnificent bird and very tame. He liked being scratched behind the ears and would seem mesmerized after a few minutes stroking. He had two major advantages as a friend over the green bird. First, he didn't bite and second he could talk. I never understood why the green head was ever brought home. He was about as nasty as a bird could get and, with a beak that he kept honed like a razor. He could really do major damage. Come to think about it maybe that's why we kept him. I think my father took some perverse pleasure in having his friends ambushed by the bird because, invariably, even though warned not to stick a finger in his cage, they would do so, and the result was immediate: a mangled digital member.

My parents were, in those days, strongly conservative republicans. Eventually my mother outgrew this disability but my father never did. During the presidential campaign, the older people tried to teach the yellow bird to say "to Hell with Roosevelt." He would squawk, say "pretty Polly, Polly wants a cracker" and other equally mundane phrases that people think parrots should say, but adamantly failed to utter the magic words. Failed, that is, until the day after the election, which Roosevelt won. All day long he kept screaming "to Hell with Roosevelt!" Once learned, a phrase was never forgotten and until the day he died he was shouting out his curse at the President.

We had a major problem with both parrots. The weather, during the winter months in southeast Pennsylvania is usually atrocious, and I can't remember a year when one or both birds didn't get colds. My Mother would dope their drinking water with some sort of jungle juice she got from the vet and while ministering to the ills would say, "poor Polly, sick as Hell." The yellow bird picked up on this very quickly because he found out that if he mimicked her by squalling in a quavering voice "poor Polly, sick as Hell" he'd get a shot of something in his water. That bird must have had a liver that looked like a football.

He had an uncanny ability to match my mother's voice. That's not to say she screeched like a parrot, although she could bellow along with the best. It's just that old Polly was a great mimic. Our family garden was behind the house about a hundred yards from the front porch. In the summer the birds, in their cages, would be put out on the porch. My grandfather, over six feet tall, was very obese. On occasions when a phone call would come for him, at a time when he would be working in the garden, my mother would step out on the porch and holler "Pop, Pop, telephone." He, naturally, would respond by leaving the garden to answer the call.

On one very hot summer day my grandfather, in the garden, heard a call to the phone and he rushed down to respond. It wasn't my mother, it was the yellow bird and as Pop hurried by his cage on the porch the bird actually laughed and called out "pretty Polly." I'm happy to say that I don't know what stuffed, roasted parrot tastes like, but we came damn close to Polly dinner that night.

That bird was the tormenter of poor old, dumb Gunny. That dog truly loved my mother and when called by her would instantly respond, eager to please. Old yellow head would mimic my mother, calling to him, and the dumb bastard would fall for it every time. He would gallop up to the porch expecting to be greeted by his favorite friend to be cruelly disappointed. The unrepentant old bird would squawk and chuckle. Fortunately for the old Dane the bird got pneumonia and flew off to his final perch before he ran the dog to death.

We are not bird people and have never gotten into canaries, budgies and the like, however, as I got into tying my own flies for fishing, I began to assemble a number of various fowl so that I would have a ready supply of feathers to harvest when needed.

To this end, I purchased 3 guinea birds, a male and two hens. They were allowed to roam freely and in the evenings, roosted in the Cyprus trees behind our home. In a very short period of time we have a large flock of these critters that totaled nearly three dozen birds. Their range took in about a half mile radius from home, but most of that area was raw, brush land and they stayed away, normally, from the neighbor's property. Normally, but not always.

Our neighbors adjacent to our home on the east side are about as fine a couple one would hope for. They take care of their property, mind their own business and give assistance whenever it is sought. However, even the most temperate of souls can be pushed too hard and my flying flock, one morning tipped the neighbors over the edge.

They have a flat, gravel roof; a type of cover that requires replacement after a time, and they had just had a complete new topping of their home which included a final layer of gravel. Just what my birds decided they needed to replenish their craws.

At six o'clock in the morning our phone rang and upon answering, I heard my neighbor hollering in mortal outrage. "Your God-damn birds are eating my roof." Clearly his outpouring of grief was justified. Think about it. Wouldn't any reasonable person be a little put off if he was awakened at some ungodly hour by three dozen flying demons pounding on his roof? It must have sounded like the rolling snare drums of the Marine Corps Band. Fortunately my flock was fed two times a day and being greedy birds, would come when called. I ended the assault on the neighbor's home by going out back and cackling for the birds that happily abandoned their gravel picking for a little cracked corn.

We had guineas back on the farm and I had learned then just how incredibly stupid they are. Foxes know how dumb these birds are. A smart fox, finding these dummies roosting in a tree, will walk around in a circle beneath the birds. The hens, twisting their heads around and around, get so dizzy they fall off their perch and flutter down where they become guinea dinner. To avoid a constant drain on our farm birds we installed a chicken wire enclosure around their favorite roosting tree, preventing the local foxes from tumbling them down. Fortunately for my later flock, they didn't have to deal with any foxes.

These farm guineas had a big old apple tree that was their favorite place to roost. It was a big flock, and much bigger than the one we had in California. There was a tune that came out during World War II, or maybe even way before, the title of which had something to do about not sitting under an apple tree. I know from personal experience that it's not even safe to walk under an apple tree. It's lucky for me that elephants don't normally roost in apple trees.

We could always tell when the guineas had completed their day's adventures. At dusk, the whole group would fly up to the tops of the Monterey Cyprus trees right behind the house. As they settled in for the evening they all started talking at once, no doubt sharing with each other whatever fascinating adventures they had experienced during the day. We would be subjected to about thirty minutes of raucous cackling and squawking. Crazy birds.

Turkey feathers, because of their rigidity, are exceptionally good for tying certain flies such as imitation grasshoppers, so I added to my ready source of supply a tom and two hen turkeys. In due course we began to receive an added benefit from the hens. Turkey eggs. I like French toast. The whole family likes French toast, which our kids dubbed as mountain toast. I've never had a better breakfast of such a meal than when turkey eggs are used in the batter. The yolks are thick and rich and, I'm sure, not on any doctors' list of things to eat. The tom, which was imaginatively named Tom, became a great pet, and when he

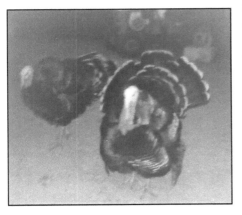

spread his tail, fanned it actually, and walked around strutting his stuff, he was truly awesome. Tom was a very friendly soul, liked being scratched on his chest and, like old yellow head, behind his ears. He gobbled the way a turkey is supposed to gobble, and did the turkey trot to impress his ladies. He got on well with all of the other animals, especially our spotted horses. We lost Tom in the end when either coyotes or a bobcat savaged him, both of which are included in the wild critters in our area. Of the two, I suspect it was a cat because Tom was big enough to go one on one with any coyote.

The last of my feathered group were a number of banty chickens, again selected for their feathers. These were primarily white Japanese silkies, who supplied exceptionally fine feathers for marabou flies. I had one rooster and whatever you've heard about banty roosters is true. His natural combativeness was increased to maniacal savagery as a result of the harvesting of a tail feather or two from time to time. The technique was to hold him with one hand, select a choice quill and pluck it out- a process that produced from such a small bird, a large cry of outrage. In time, this bird decided that there wasn't the least possibility that he and I could enter into any sort of reasonable relationship or friendship and his hatred was indeed intense. When I think about it, I have to accept that he was fully justified. I suspect if some damn big, giant regularly picked me up and plucked hairs from my butt that I would not thank him for it. The little demon had a pair of very, very sharp spurs and I had to wear a pair of heavy leather gauntlets when I went for a plucking. He was so mean spirited that I had to segregate him from his ladies. He was the smallest, biggest bully I've ever known and a dedicated wife beater. Given a chance, he would beat his girls bloody. We never did get any chicks out of the hens and it's a small wonder. It's a little hard to think about serious sex and romance after you've had the hell kicked out of you. As a lover he was a total flop. He met his match one night when a weasel managed to get into the bird's pen and that was that.

About mid-way into the chicken program, I got a pair of Polish crested chickens. My memory is that the 'City Girl' was the main mover on these birds, and I can't fault her. Our rooster was a magnificent feathered friend. As chickens go he was about mid-sized. His plumage was coal black, except for his top knot. The whole top of his head was crowned with a big puff of snow white feathers. My wife named him Count Pulaski. He was such a neat looking bird I couldn't bring myself to pluck feathers to tie flies with so I just gathered whatever quality quills he dropped around the yard.

Now this was a roo that was very vain. He knew he was the best looking cock on the ground. Strut! That bird could strut sitting down. He had a very distinctive crow and even with six or so assorted roosters, when he lit off it was easy to pick him out. It's kind of nice to hear roosters crowing in the early morning at dawn when the first light is breaking. The trouble with the Count is that he was Polish and he would cork off a cook-a-doodle anytime from midnight on. You sure as hell couldn't set your watch by him.

When we were first married, we lived for a time in an apartment available for married students. Dogs, cats and such were not permitted, so we got into a modest, five gallon aquarium with assorted tropical fish. There's not much personality in a fish, perhaps that's why some folks are referred to as "a cold fish."

They are fascinating to watch and there's something sort of relaxing just sitting, watching them swooze around in their tank.

Our problem is that one tank wasn't enough. By the end of the year we had five, ten and twenty gallon tanks, plus a beta display tank. The betas, also called Siamese fighting fish, are among the most spectacular of the fresh water fishes, and when preening for a fight, or to romance a lady, they are awesome.

Their sex life became a major event in the apartment and often, when we were mating a pair, our living room would be packed with sexual voyeurs watching the show. It was the fifties version of a pornographic movie.

Our first attempts to get baby betas were total failures and ended with the males killing their females. The basic procedure was to take a five gallon tank with nothing in it other than about two inches of water. No plants, no gravel, no filter, just plain nothing.

Betas are air breathers and bubble nesters. The male is the nest builder. He achieves this by blowing little bubbles until he creates a frothy nest about two inches in diameter and maybe a half inch thick. During mating the male wraps himself around the lady fish and squeezes the eggs out of her, fertilizing them with his milch as they drop to the bottom of the tank. Once he's wrung her dry it's best to remove her immediately because if not, he'll normally kill her. Male betas are pretty rough lovers. Anyway, with the lady removed, the male picks up the eggs and spits them into the bubbles. It takes about forty-eight hours for the fish to hatch out.

As I indicated, our initial efforts never got to the wrapping and squeezing part of their romancing because we had things backwards.

In the beginning we'd put the male into the tank first and let him get used to it. Once we saw that he was starting a nest we'd pop in a lady fish that would invariably be killed within twenty-four hours. Suddenly, it occurred to us that the male wasn't taking "I've got a headache" as a reason to avoid romance. Now men, take this seriously. It's a good idea to make sure the lady's in the right frame of mind before you make your move.

We turned repeated disasters into a one hundred percent success story by reversing the process. First we put the lady in the breeding tank and let her get comfortably adapted to her boudoir. After a week, to ten days we would divide the bedroom with a sheet of clear window glass, then plop the male in on one side with the lady on the other. It was sort of a modern day equivalent of a bundling board. The result was many, many baby betas.

We had to keep the males separated from each other as well as our other fish because of their innate desire to bite everything else that swam. There's a special tank that separates six males by glass panels. It allows them to see each other which causes them to spread their fins and go through their pre-fight bragging. It's not too much different than what you see between two boxers at ring center before the first bell.

While the finny friends didn't have individual personalities, each particular variety had individual characteristics more or less particular to that species. These differences made just watching a mixed tank a lot of fun. Two species that were favorites of the 'City Girl' were scats and puffers, both of whom are somewhat comical, especially the puffers. Unfortunately we were never able to keep them for any length of time. I suspect that was because our tanks were totally fresh water and both of these species prefer a little salinity.

There was another couple in the building who were close friends of ours and who also got into keeping tropical fish. They had an apartment one floor above ours. Eventually they had a huge, one hundred gallon tank. As I recall, they had gotten it second hand. It developed a small leak in one corner about two-thirds of the way down and my good buddy figured the way to stop it was to push on the glass from inside the tank. With the pressure of a hundred gallons of water plus his extra pounds, the glass was overloaded and the panel fractured, pouring water and fish all over the floor. This required mounting out a major rescue operation with all of us trying to pick fish out of the rug and get them downstairs to our tanks before they died. In the meantime, there was a hundred gallons or so of water that, being ignored, made its own way down stairs through the walls and ceilings. Good news! My memory is that we were able to save virtually all of the fish. The walls didn't fare as well.

After graduation, we broke down all of the aquariums, picked out our best fish, which included all the betas and headed for New England. Since then, off and on, we've started up a small tank but for the most part we've not returned to keeping topical fish. They are too prone to a variety of nasty diseases like fungus, ich rot, whatever and once that stuff gets started, it's hard to get rid of.

What we have are a bunch of ponds and, in the big one, which holds about three thousand gallons, we have some very nice koi, along with bull frogs, mud turtles, crayfish, and large goldfish. The pond is filtered and aerated by a stream and water falls that are powered by a circulating pump. It's very relaxing to sit out by the pond at dusk with a glass of Chardonnay in hand and toss pellets to the fish. The koi are a mixed batch with very vivid red, orange, black and white markings. Some bi-colored, some tri-colored, and some almost calico. These are big fish and they drive Duke crazy. A couple of them are damn near as big as he is and for the life of him, he hasn't been able to figure out a way to turn them into a dinner.

The only two problems we've had have been the result of a little poaching from some local low-life wildlife. Specifically, raccoons and a large blue heron, locally known as Freddy. The coons have had limited success but have gotten one or two of the smaller fish and since it is a delicacy to them, I would guess a crayfish from time to time.

Freddy is another matter altogether. We've got some pretty neat neighbors across the street that also have a large fish pond with koi. Freddy's initial depredations were against their fish. Ultimately they erected a protective netting that seriously interfered with his fishing, so he started visiting our pond. It's not as accessible as the neighbors' pond had been, so it took old Freddy a while to get up his courage and to figure out a way to land so as to access the pond. He's a big sucker and on the ground is easily over three feet tall with a beak like a Spanish dueling foil. I know he got one of the larger comets because he left a few scales, a little blood, and a lot of bird scat on the slab where he polished the fish off.

Now, as a general rule, I'm pretty supportive of the native critters and understand their natural habits and needs. However, I took exception to Freddy's raids on my ponds. He's got miles of swamps, lagoons, tidal streams and the like to do his fishing and the only reason I could figure out for his hitting on us was that the damn bird is lazy. Years ago, when I first went to Colorado, I remember this place where they had a big trout pond and you could rent a pole and catch a fish. It was truly fishing in a barrel. Well, damn it, that's just what Freddy was doing. He was fishing in my barrel. I didn't want to kill the sucker so we tried scaring him off. I used a fake owl. Freddy wanted to shake hands with it. We tossed small stones at him. He'd flutter over to the neighbors, wait until he thought all was clear, and back he would come. It became obvious that Freddy and I needed to have a meeting of the minds, and given the size of a bird's brain, even at Freddy's size, you can bet that I was beginning to get an inferiority complex over not being able to outsmart him.

The way it finally worked out is I got a sling shot. We have a bunch of macadamia nut trees, and I selected a pouch full of smaller nuts, about the size of a large pea, and waited for Freddy to raid the homestead. I had practiced a little with the shooter, but you can bet I was no David.

Anyway, one Saturday morning I peeked out the window that fronts our patio and spied old Freddy on the other side of our swimming pool, calmly strolling towards one of the smaller ponds that held the goldfish. I loaded up my rubber gun and jumped out onto the patio, with a loud shout. Freddy, about thirty feet away, started hopping along, beating his wings, to get airborne. When he'd made it about four feet in the air, I cut down on him with the sling shot and damn if I didn't hit him in the right tit. He let out a loud squawk, did a left handed chandelle and flew off into the wild blue. That's the last we've seen of Freddy. Naturally, when I told my son of nailing Freddy on the wing he was a little skeptical, but eventually, reluctantly accepted that I had indeed caught Freddy on the rise. After all, is was the only sporting thing to do.

The 'City Girl' is an instinctive naturalist and a great lover of nature's children. However, notwithstanding the fact that she was bestowed a Bachelor of Science degree from a very fine Eastern university, she flunked basic biology at home.

Late one afternoon as I arrived home from work, the lady was bubbling over about the remarkable rescue that had taken place in our swimming pool earlier in the afternoon. She had walked out onto the patio and saw a large toad swimming around in the pool with a little toad on its back. Since the pool is chlorinated, she dip-netted the pair and put them in the big fish pond. She just couldn't say enough good things about the bravery and devotion of the big toad in saving its little friend from drowning.

The next morning we had about ten thousand toad eggs, linked in strings, all over the surface of the pond. Our children gave her a crash lecture on the birds, the bees and butterflies with a little extra about toads.

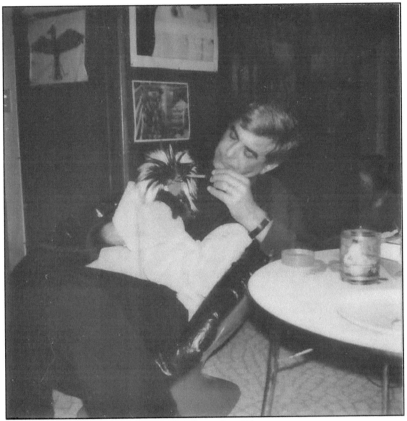

Nursing his Polish Rooster back to health

Chapter 10: The Paloose Ponies

When I left the farm to go west to college I left behind me, with a great feeling of relief, any desire to ever be burdened again with the care of horses. At age eighteen I had close to fifteen years of experience with these less than bright friends and it seemed at the time more than enough. I had been bitten, stepped on, rolled on, dumped on the ground and as a matter of fact, received from horses the only serious injuries I had suffered up to that point of my life. I had accumulated a broken jaw, broken ribs, a fractured arm and numerous minor cuts, bruises and sundry humiliations. I had curried enough hides, forked out enough manure and wet straw, spent hours riding cold mornings to satisfy a life time. Had I been asked whether or not I desired to engage in the care, culture and keep of a horse in the future I would have safely answered, like the Raven, "never more."

When our first born, my daughter, reached the age of six, or seven, she was bitten by the horse bug. This particular insect attacks young girls far more often than young boys. It took me awhile before I understood this phenomenon. The answer is simple. You need to perceive a six year old girl-child, who weighs maybe fifty pounds, sitting on top of an eight hundred to thousand pound dumb animal, bullying the hell out of it. It comes natural to them. It's part of their basic training

because ultimately it equips them for married life; and the lessons learned in bullying their horses they apply to their husbands. Mother Nature does indeed have a mean streak.

Anyway, when my little joy of life began to badger me about getting a horse my immediate reactions were horror, rejection and obfuscation. Faced with a persistent and obstinate little person, I raised a series of what I think were ingenuous diversions and roadblocks, all of which had the lasting power of a sand castle at the beach when the tide is on the rise. Having been thoroughly out-maneuvered, I finally became the beneficiary of what I believed to be an absolutely fail-safe solution. One of our neighbors' daughters, who had a Connemara pony "Imperial Kaiser" about fourteen hands high, had reached the age of sixteen. Her interests were then turning to boys and I have no doubts she was burning with the desire to inflict upon these objects of her attention, the bullying tactics she had perfected with her pony. Whatever, she had infected my daughter with the horse bug and the two spent a lot of time together with the pony, Impy. Badgered beyond belief, I finally made a deal with my daughter. With the neighbor's consent, she would take over full care of the pony. They would pay for its feed, vet care and other expenses, but my daughter would feed it twice a day, clean out the corral, exercise it daily and curry its hide and clean its hooves. The deal was that if Lisa, my daughter, proved that she could do this for one year, I would get her a horse of her own, whose care she would be fully responsible for. Because I made it painfully clear, I was not going to get back into the horse business.

Well, it's no guess what happened. Lisa was absolutely dedicated to the deal and met her end of the bargain even while recovering from a broken arm that resulted from a fall, while riding the neighbor's nag.

At the end of the year I had no arguments left. It takes a bigger rogue than I am to welsh on a deal with one's own child, so we started out horse hunting. Fortunately, we lived in a rural area and had plenty of space to build a corral, covered stall, feed shed and the like so that once Lisa had selected her horse it could be kept right behind the house.

For very little cost, we purchased a three year old appaloosa mare. We named her Tahnamia, which translates into Pretty Walker. She was big, burly and green as hell. I didn't care, my daughter was ecstatic, she could now join with her friends and ride for miles on her own nag and I didn't have to do a thing, other than buy a little hay, grain, pay vet bills, farrier bills and outfit Lisa with tack, western gear and the like. I thought it a bargain as long as I didn't have to do anything else like shovel manure, feed, etc.

Tahni was a snow-flaked appy. That's to say she was basically a

solid dun, roan color with small white spots all over with a frosting on her rump. The most common appy's are blanket colored. Normally a solid dark with a snow white blanket over their hind quarters that will have dark spots. The most spectacular of this breed are the leopard members whose basic coat is white and spotted with numerous dark spots, red, brown or black.

These horses were a specialty of Nez Perce Indians in Idaho and are generally prized for their stamina and sure-footedness. As a rule, they are gentle, quiet and easily trained.

Unfortunately, cross-breeding with quarter horses has produced appy's that are fat, chunky and not good for much other than running around in show rings, in equitation classes. They are far removed from the traditional paloose ponies that could navigate over mountainous terrain and cover many miles, daily.

Lisa worked hard in training Tahni and after about a year began to enter her in the local horse shows, learning a little from each, and with rising success. Tahni would never win an equine Miss America contest, but she did develop into a better than average trail horse and, in such events, Lisa began to pick up some ribbons. Everybody was

happy, Lisa, the horse and me. About a year after Lisa acquired Tahni, she had her entered into a major regional show that was held a little over a mile from our home. As was usual, the whole family went to give moral support to our girls, Tahni and Lisa; plus which we really enjoyed these events. We got to see a lot of really quality hay burners. This particular show was a three day affair, Friday through Sunday. Lisa's first class was scheduled for Saturday morning so we had missed all of Friday's doings, which included the halter classes for yearlings.

In between Lisa's first two classes, I was walking around the barn area, looking at the variety of spotted nags that had come from all over the southwest. Lord, I should have stayed in bed. Rounding a corner I saw, double hitched to a wash stand, a seven month old snorty horse. He was magnificent. He looked to be about thirteen to fourteen hands. His body was a light marly blue with a beautiful snow white blanket on his butt that was liberally sprinkled with black and brown leopard spots. It was obvious that, in addition to his appaloosa breeding, he had a lot of arabian blood to look back on. As it turned out, he was double registered.

He had a fully appy registration and a separate, half arab registration. My eyeballs began revolving in opposite directions and by noon the next day, he was mine. I was back in the horse business.

Since we lived relatively close by, I couldn't see any reason to have him trailered to our place. It was simple, I'd just put a halter on him and lead him home, easy and quick. Sure it was. Snorty had been cooped up in a small show stall for the best part of three days and was full of oats. The first half of a mile required leading him along the side of a heavily travelled country road, including taking him under a major over-pass for an interstate highway.

He may have only been a seven month old baby, but I guarantee you he was an active little sucker and had more hops than a flea. With all of the backings and forwards and side to side moves that little stroll home ended up being closer to five miles. I don't ever remember being so exhausted.

I re-named him Insula, which translates into "Little Chief," and we called him Sula for short. Sula had it all. His appaloosa coloring was striking and, while registered as a half Arab he was, in actuality, a three-quarter Arabian.

I should explain something. Appaloosas are a color breed, as are palominos, paints and pintos. In the case of appaloosas, to qualify for registration they must display certain, recognizable color characteristics. These include the spotted hides, laminated hooves where the horn will show dark stripes, and white stripes, parti-colored skin around their eyes, nostrils or genitals and a white ring, or sclera around their eyes. Certain horses, such as thoroughbreds, Arabians, Morgans, etc. are registered by blood lines. It is therefore possible, by selective breeding, to get horses that can be registered by bloodline and color.

Sula's Arab blood was easily discernible. He had the typical dish face and tulip ears. He had a full, thick, flowing mane and tail, and the total result was a very striking horse.

Unfortunately, he joined us with a bad habit that we were never able to break. He had pretty much been the family pet on the ranch where he had been foaled and had been, as kids can be, spoiled rotten. He liked to grab things in his mouth, a not uncommon trait for stud horses and not something anyone would want to encourage. What may seem cute in a colt can be downright dangerous in a grown stallion. What he liked to do was firmly grip a hand with his teeth and slobber. At seven months it was no big deal, at three years he could give real pain.

Anyway, having established the conditions and rules for horse ownership, I was in no position of strength to dump on my daughter the chore of taking care of my horse, so we evenly divided up the chores. I didn't want to start Sula into being ridden until he was close to three. Full grown, he went a little over fifteen hands and while he had a deep powerful chest and barrel, I didn't want to run any risk to hurting his soft young bones. When it came time to break him in, I took him over to a friend who specialized in gently breaking youngsters, especially colts,

and after about three months, Sula came home, green broken, diploma and all. I had ridden him often during the last month on the training farm but always under control of a fenced area or walled training ring. The day I got him back, I decided to ride him bare-backed around the track we had cut out of the native brush behind the house. I figured that I would get a better feel for his moves without a saddle and I was right. He had a lot of moves and I got to feel all of them. After an hour's work-out, I rubbed him down, and turned him back into his corral. He had worn two dollar sized sores on my butt, one on each cheek, that took a month to heal. For two weeks I had to go around with pads on my rear so that I wouldn't weep through my britches.

With Sula and Tahni now broken for riding some of the best years I have enjoyed with my daughter commenced. On weekends we could ride for hours, taking a light lunch, and something for our spotted friends in our saddlebags. There were miles and miles of trails to enjoy and explore, and always training days to prepare for shows.

Originally, I had intended to use Sula as a stud for a small group of three or four mares and with these friends embark on an appy breeding venture with my daughter. I suppose I was using the same thought process that resulted in our ending up with three poodles. Get some babies on the ground and get our money back. With Sula it didn't work out that way and when he was five I had him gelded. The major reason was that he had inherited a greying gene which is a very undesirable characteristic in an appaloosa. It is a trait associated with Arabs and as the horse matures, if it has the gene, between the ages of five to ten years, it loses its color. Ultimately, in Sula's case, he turned mostly white- no blanket, few spots. That's murder for a paloose pony. The second reason he was cut was that since I couldn't use him for a herd pappy there was no reason to run the risks of all of the nasty dangerous tricks a snorty horse pulls. At the time, I referred to the operation as "brain surgery" involving a double, lower lobotomy.

Prior to the cutting, we had gotten one foal out of Tahni, by Sula. She was a filly but of unremarkable coloring. She registered as an appy but did not inherit her daddy's vibrant markings. She took after her mamma. The

act of conception occurred when Sula, not yet three, had been sexually harassed by Tahni. Sula had not reached full size but somehow with Tahni's assistance he got into her part of the corral. I had gotten home from work and had walked out back where I heard a commotion from the corrals. What I found was my twelve year old daughter and a friend about the same age with whom she rode mesmerized by advanced equine sex. Tahni was more than ready for a little romance, for that matter, so was Sula. They had one major problem. She was close to sixteen hands and he hadn't gotten much over fourteen. He needed a step ladder. I don't know how long they had been trying to consummate their love, but it hadn't worked out. Sula had all the right equipment, as evidenced by the big-eyed stares of two pre-teen girls, except height. I decided that what was needed was the assistance of an older, wiser man, because it was obvious that Sula's boyish impetuosity was going to result in a long, frustrating afternoon. I hitched Tahni to a post, put a halter on snorty and let him stand behind her breathing the exciting perfume that she had that day until he was trembling with rapture. This also gave him a chance to get some strength back into his legs. Finally, when I felt he was ready to jump over the moon, I backed him up about eight feet, swatted him on the butt and let him at her. As he jumped, I whisked her tail out of the

way and he nailed her, with all four feet off the ground. It was truly a flying you know what.

About six months before Sula's surgery, Lisa and I had trailered over to a ranch where a friend of ours was boarding two of his horses. One, a very pretty appy mare (Coconut) and the other a coal black, full Arabian stud (Abraxas) who just happened to be one of the most well behaved, snorty horses I've ever known, especially when compared to Sula who could be rasty as hell. The friend had a nephew visiting from New York whose last contact with a horse had been one with the name "hobby" in front of "horse". Because of that we put him on Tahni who, all things considered, was the most docile and tractable of the four. Lisa rode the other appy mare, I had Sula and my friend his arab. The ride was a simple walk-about, up and down some gentle hills, through some valleys, a total of five or six miles. It was, until nearly the very end, uneventful, when all hell broke loose. Sweet, gentle Tahni started it, which, when you think about it, should surprise no one. Females are the cause of most of the trouble on this earth whatever species they belong to. Just before the end of our ride, we had to cross a small shallow stream. Every one of those horses had been trained to go through water and had done so time and again without any fuss. Tahni, at this point in the ride, had easily worked it out that she had a rank greenhorn on her back and decided to have a little fun. She stopped at the stream as if it contained the Loch Ness monster and snorting and jumping, hopped over it. The rest of us were maybe fifty feet down the trail. When the greener and Tahni caught up with us, he complained because she had popped him so abruptly in getting over the creek, he had lost a lens out of his glasses. I swung Sula around and went back to look for it leaving, I thought, the other three down the trail. All during the ride Sula made it very clear that he was displeased with having another stud along but other than a head toss or snort, he kept himself under control. About three feet short of the creek I saw the lens in a tuft of grass, unbroken. I hollered to the rest that I had found it, swung off Sula and bent down to pick it up. What I didn't know was that my good buddy had trailed me back on his stud to join the search.

All Sula needed to get a shot at the Arab was me off his back. He clued me in with a piercing scream of rage as he reared on his hind legs, spinning to assault the other stud. I tried to jerk him down with the reins when he clipped me behind the ear with a foot, grabbed me and flipped me in the bushes. Totally out of control, he jumped the Arab from the rear who, incidentally, had wanted no part of any fracas, grabbed my friend by the left upper arm, dragging him from the saddle, all while trying to pound the other horse with his front feet. The Arab took off under an oak tree with my snorter raging behind him. Sula hooked his saddle horn on a low limb of the oak while the other stud escaped. Sula had acorns, leaf mold and twigs flying all over the place. By this time both my friend and I had recovered- he had caught up with his horse and I had captured Sula who was still hooked up with the oak tree. With both of us back in the saddle the fracas was over and other than some snorting and prancing, we rode back to the trailer area without

further trouble. However, my daughter had ridden ahead to get some first aid supplies, which were not available, and all of the little girls on the ranch came riding down to get a firsthand accounting of the big fight. Now, at

this point, I was mad, hurt and bleeding, and not a little scared. I knew enough about horses to know that we had been lucky. I knew my friend had a messed up arm, and the last thing I wanted was any more horse trouble on that day, and here comes a whole cavalry troop of squealing little girls. I ran them out of the immediate area of our trailer, using language I hadn't heard since the Marine Corps. Sula was all hypered up again and we had one hell of a time getting him loaded into the trailer so that we could get home. After his subsequent "brain surgery" we didn't have any more frolics of this sort and, for the first time, I could let my daughter ride and train him. Lisa, who had become a first rate trainer, turned Sula into one of the best trail competitors in our area and, riding him, earned some serious awards.

Disaster struck one weekend when we found Tahni suffering from a severe colic. Minor ailments we could handle, but not a problem of that nature. The vet's diagnosis was sand colic. Tahni was a voracious feeder and would vacuum up every last flake of alfalfa or the last kernel of grain. Unfortunately, she also sucked up a lot of sand along with everything else. That sand collected in her large intestines and packed up, producing a belly ache of monumental proportions. When a severe pain would hit her she would drop as if she had been pole axed and try to roll. We couldn't let her do that for fear that, by rolling on the ground, her gut would loop and that would finish her. Lisa and I nursed her for nearly three days, 24 hours a day, around the clock. Four hours on and four hours off. We gave her shots for pain and to relax the spasms. We tube fed her mucillose and kept her walking continuously, except when the pain knocked her down. Our vet visited twice a day and quietly told me I had better prepare Lisa for bad news. Nothing was moving out of that mare and the Doc didn't believe she'd make it. By the third day, I wasn't sure any of us would. Lisa and I had become walking zombies. Sula just couldn't figure out what was happening with all of the activity and flood lights on all night. Finally, noon the third day, the mucillose began to work and Tahni began to pass out the sand, buckets of it. The relief that came to us was terminated immediately. Sula, somehow, had hooked a large nail that was imbedded in a rail in his teeth, broke his jaw and did major damage to his gums when he jerked his head. Damn, I cried. Back came the vet. Here we had just pulled Tahni back from the brink and now Sula was in a mess. We had to knock him down with a shot of dope so that our vet could put a screw in his jaw bone, wire it together and stitch him up. He didn't have much of an appetite for anything, especially nails, for nearly a week. Four times a day we had to rinse his mouth out with an antiseptic douche solution plus stick him with antibiotic shots. These consecutive disasters reminded me why I had decided I was through with horses when I left the farm.

My daughter, by the time she reached thirteen, was a first rate horsewoman. She had a natural ability and really loved working with them and training for shows. We rode together as much as possible, especially on weekends. One Saturday, I came close to losing my daughter. We were exercising Tahni and Sula in an open area of over a hundred acres behind the house. I had Sula and was ponying the young filly while Lisa worked her mare. We had just broken them into a gentle lope when Tahni got her front feet tangled up, stumbled and flipped. I was maybe twenty feet behind them and all I saw, initially, was a cloud of dust and Tahni's big butt flipping over. I knew Lisa had ended up on the bottom and truly believed she was badly hurt, if not killed. I knew real terror for the first time in my life. I jumped off Sula and dove into the dust.

Incredibly, lady luck was with us. Lisa was lying, pinned under Tahni's belly, between her front and rear legs. Initially, the mare was stunned and lying quietly so that by the time I got to her and was able to calm her down, she had not struggled or tried to rise. If she had, she would have tromped on Lisa for sure. The trouble was, I couldn't get Lisa's leg free to drag her out of danger. I hollered for help but we were too far from any homes and no one heard me. Somehow, and I can't say how, I was finally able to heave enough on Tahni and pull on Lisa so that her foot came out of her boot, and she was freed. Other than a brush burn and minor bruises she was fine. Tahni had some small cuts and bruises but she too was alright. We took the group back home, rubbed them down, and went into the house. That's when I began to shake. I trembled as if I had Saint Vitus dance. That was the first time that I had ever seen one of my own in real peril and it shook Old Dad to his toes. The lesson is that there is always potential danger riding horses and if you get into it you'd better be prepared to have some bad times. They are big, dumb animals and can hurt you.

Sula liked to play tricks. The bad habit he had of grabbing things with his mouth had gotten him into serious trouble when he broke his jaw but it didn't really teach the dummy a thing. He still liked to nip.

One Sunday we were out back just fooling around the corrals, cleaning tack, washing and grooming our friends. At that time, we had a large, very fluffy, yellow tom cat who my wife named Taffy. Taffy had ambled out with us and had jumped up on top of one of the 4 x 4 cedar corner posts in the corral. He perched with his back to the inside of the fence, swishing his truly magnificent bushy tail. It was simply more than Sula could stand. He snuck up on Taffy and grabbed him firmly at the base of his tail with his front teeth. Taffy was doing a hundred miles an hour going nowheres on top of that post, shredding splinters and wood chips all over the place, howling with indignation. Sula got an owlish look on his face and wouldn't let go. Finally, when I had stopped laughing, had dried my eyes, and could function, I pried Sula's jaws open so that old puss could escape. He looked like a moon shot coming off that post.

Sula had a few other tricks which were not at all fun. When being brushed and curried, if you were up around his front, he would whip his head around and nip you on the butt. Then, if you moved back towards his rear to get away from being fanged he would try a cow-kick. Since at the time I had not yet gelded him I needed to be careful about how I put a stop to his shenanigans. Stallions can have long memories and will get revenge on anyone they feel deserves punishing. I did not want to put those types of thoughts in his ornery little brain, so I had to come up with some tricks of my own to discourage his pranks, using methods he wouldn't blame on me.

First I worked on his fancy foot work to put an end to being cow-kicked. I took him into the middle of the pasture and snugged him with a three legged hobble, then, I started grooming him, standing where he just knew he could nail me. When he popped his left-hind leg forward to get me, he yanked his feet right out from under himself and flopped on the ground. I loosened the hobbles and let him up, then snugged them down again and resumed my brushing. He tried again, same result. He couldn't blame me because he could see I hadn't made a move when he tried to kick. An hour later and about ten trips to the deck finally convinced him that he was in a no win game and he gave it up. That left me with curing his nip. I cut a piece of baling wire, made two loops that fit over the middle fingers of my left hand with the two ends protruding about an inch out from my fist. These I had honed down until they were needle points. They fit sort of like brass knuckles.

I started brushing him, standing within easy range of a nip, but holding my left hand, with the wire tips pointed forwards so that if, as I was sure he would, he tried a bite, he would run his tender nose right on the points. I didn't have to move. It worked like a charm. The first shot he tried stung like twin hornets. After about six attempts you could almost hear his brain churning. His ears were working back and forth and he sort of peeked sideways to see if it was something I was doing. I just kept on working with the brush. I just knew he was going to try again, which he did, with the same result. I hadn't made a move on him and his snout, by now very sore, got spiked again. With an audible sigh, he gave it up. You have no idea what an ego trip it is to find out that you're smarter than a horse.

Insula ("Little Chief")

Riding Tahnamia (Pretty Walker) in Native American dress

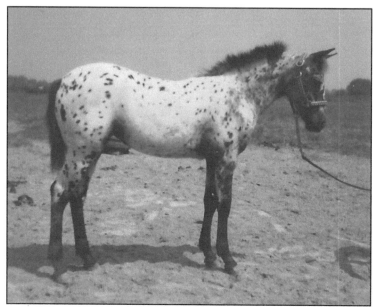

Spotted Feather (Kangi Gleska) aka "Boots" as a filly

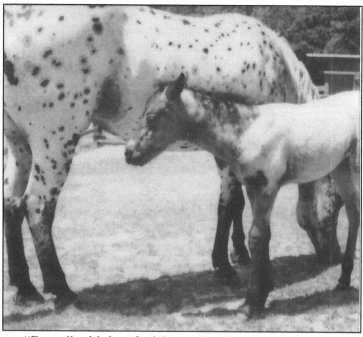

"Boots" with her foal Spotted Wind (Tade Gleska)

Show Time!

Trail Class with Insula- sidepass over a bale of straw without touching it!

Peta Witco (Crazy Fire) aka "Red"

Tahnis foal Waptastamana (Black Feather), Boots, Insula, Tahnamia

Chapter 11: Goodbye Scotty

We are down to two house friends as I write this final chapter. Duke, loyal soul that he is, is still with us. His fickle sister, Possum, was catnapped by a neighbor across the street. What actually happened is that our daughter visited with our twin, one year old, grandsons. Possum took one look at those little terrors and left permanently. She was already displeased with the roughneck tactics of her brother, Duke, and must have decided that the additional burden of the twins was adding insult to injury. Whatever, she's not been home since and I miss her.

Sueme, my rare Tasmanian lion killer (there's only one in the entire world), is the second home soul. She's only about ten inches tall, and weighs maybe twenty pounds. However, she sounds like a pack of Siberian wolves, and as long as visitors are on the other side of a door, she's ferocious. Once strangers are in the house, it's another matter entirely. As watchdogs go, she's a complete wimp, and hides in whatever is the most convenient, least accessible place she can get to. Small children seem to give her the nervous twits and she wasn't a whole lot happier with the twins than Possum was, but Sueme has the dead loyal integrity that nearly all dogs have and that most cats do not, Duke being an exception. Sueme's a lot like her daddy was, with enough poodle to give her a lot of smarts. She's a very feminine, sweet natured mixture of God knows what. She has a smile, actually a grin that could get her top billing for a tooth paste commercial. Fortunately, for me, she came along in time to fill a major void

These memories of my various friends cover a span of sixty years and as a result, and also because of the wide varieties among those friends, I have formed opinions and preferences. Among all of these critters, dogs clearly out-class the rest. I can recall only very short periods during the past years when I was not blessed with one or more dogs, and I can't imagine a life without them. I don't differentiate between mutts or pure breeds. They all pretty much have the same fundamental qualities of love, loyalty, and smarts.

Cats would be next and I suppose since they, along with dogs, are pretty much in-house friends that it's natural to rank these two types at the top of the list. However, cats just don't come up to scratch when compared with a good dog.

Pete, of the French collection, and Scotty, my blue merle Aussie, sit on the top of all my friends. Pete was probably the smarter of the two, but over-all, Scotty has the edge.

Scotty, who I loved and believe to be right on top of my list of the best of all my friends, developed cancer and, as it progressed, became  more and more debilitated. He did not appear to be in any pain, but it was obvious that his strength was being sapped. Towards the end, I knew what I should have done and I kept putting it off as something for tomorrow. I was not prepared to be the moving party to his execution. As a result, I paid, as did Scotty, a fearsome penalty. Early, each morning, I start the day feeding Big Red her ration of carrots and hay. The route to her corral takes me into our patio and past our swimming pool. Normally, Scotty would be with me while I doled out Red's feed. On that last morning, as I left the house, I found Scotty, dead, in the pool. He had, evidently, fallen in, and with his ailment was too weak to get out, and had drowned. It should not have happened and, but for my cowardice in failing to let him be gently put to sleep, would not have happened.

I picked Scotty out of the pool and buried him by the path to the corrals. I suppose it seems maudlin, but at least I get to tell him "Good morning" as I do my morning chores. In every sense, this book is dedicated to that dog. He was the best of friends.

"Old Blue, you good dog you."

Epilogue:

Scotty and Sueme were not the end of my Fathers long line of friends. Sueme lived to a ripe old age, and as she got older decided she needed to stash a large number of bones- perhaps for her doggy retirement? We will never know her reasoning but somehow she decided the fireplace ashes were THE place to hide her stash… this caused a great deal of doggy-distress when Fall would come and dad would light a fire. Sueme got pretty frantic watching her life savings go up in flames and soon learned to put her valuables in a different bank

Soon after Sueme passed, Dad acquired two of the sweetest friends he would ever have. Feather, his Australian Shepard puppy, was a tricolor Aussie and stole his heart as no other pet I ever witnessed. She was always by his side, an obedient and loving dog, fiercely loyal and a great judge of character. Feather was instrumental

in obtaining a feline friend… a small, abandoned yellow tom kitten was discovered in bad shape under Dads woodpile. Dad and Feather nursed him back to health and naturally he got named "Woody". Feather mothered him like he was her own get. Like so many cats in our coyote filled area, Woody disappeared one day. Feather was sad so Dad went to the animal shelter and got a new kitten "Miss Kit" who was and still is pretty much feral. She may deign to come sit on your lap and then seconds later may decide to scratch the crap out of you. The

only one she tolerates is my Father (all the animals love Dad- even the super-nasty Nubian Goat he left out of the story… the very wrongly named Chastity who forced everyone but Dad to be armed with a squirt gun in self-defense should they dare to trespass on her territory …which consisted of the entire back acre of their property)

When Feather passed at the age of 18, it should have been a quiet, gentle passing. Sadly it didn't happen that way and I will not go into details…enough to say Dad was beyond distraught without his

canine best friend- swore he'd never have another dog… good thing we knew better and steered him in the direction of San Diego Aussie Rescue. He was soon the owner of an Aussie/Border Collie cross named Rosie. Rosie had been found starving, mange-ridden and abandoned in one of the poorer sections of San Diego County. She is now fully restored to health and, as an older dog, is happy to snooze in the patio or by Dads' side, with occasional trips over to the neighbors for a walk or visit with their dog Rosebud. In my household, we have my two English Cream Golden Retrievers- whom Dad regards as family also.

Never a call or email goes by without giving an update on "his grand-puppies" Trixie Hobbitses and Jiraiya. I'm so thankful I was raised by parents that love animals and taught me to appreciate their priceless place in our lives.